Album of
Rocks and Minerals

ALBUM OF ROCKS AND MINERALS

FROM THE BEAUTY of a sparkling diamond to the impenetrable "magic" of lead, rocks and minerals have always played a major role in human life. Just as our primitive ancestors used them for both survival and pleasure, we use rocks and minerals today. Thousands of years ago, primitive peoples started their fires by striking flint and iron and painted their cave walls with a thick paint made from hematite. Today, our lighters are based on the same "flint and iron" principle those prehistoric peoples discovered, and we still paint with hematite. The mineral halite is an essential part of our diet. Some of our greatest works of art are created with calcite. Our telephones contain pieces of specially cut quartz. And without the ore sphalerite, music just wouldn't sound the same. Through the ongoing processes that form rocks and minerals, the earth continues to provide us with these essentials of life.

Tom McGowen relates these and other exciting facts as he explores the fascinating world of rocks and minerals. Beginning with an introductory section on the formation of our rocky earth, the ALBUM OF ROCKS AND MINERALS goes on to explain how specific rocks and minerals were formed, why they look the way they do, and their many uses, both past and present. In all, fifty-five of our most important rocks and minerals and their various forms are covered. To assist the reader, an index and a pronunciation guide are included at the back of the book, following an illustrated reference section, "More Rocks and Minerals." Rod Ruth's vibrant illustrations accompany the text, giving a close-up, full-color view of eighty-one subjects and providing an aid in identifying various rocks and minerals.

The expertise and ability of the author/illustrator team of Tom McGowen and Rod Ruth are well known.

Album of Rocks and Minerals

By TOM McGOWEN

Illustrated by ROD RUTH

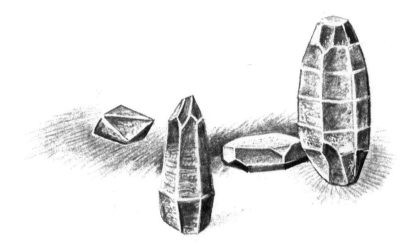

CHECKERBOARD PRESS

New York

Cover Illustrations:

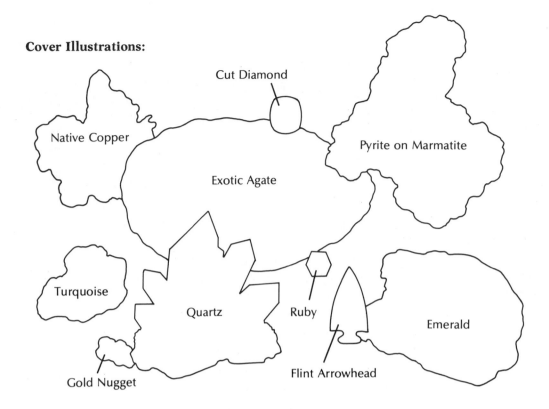

Cut Diamond

Native Copper

Pyrite on Marmatite

Exotic Agate

Turquoise

Quartz

Ruby

Emerald

Gold Nugget

Flint Arrowhead

Text and illustrations reviewed and authenticated by Dr. Edward J. Olsen, Curator of Mineralogy, Field Museum of Natural History, Chicago, Illinois

Library of Congress Cataloging-in-Publication Data
McGowen, Tom.
  Album of rocks and minerals.
  Reprint. Originally published: © 1981.
  Includes index.
  Summary: Describes the formation and uses of the
world's leading minerals.
  1. Mineralogy—Juvenile literature. 2. Rocks—
Juvenile literature. [1. Mineralogy] I. Ruth,
Rod, ill. II. Title.
QE432.2.M33 1987   549   86–31757
ISBN 0–02–688511–5 (hardcover)
ISBN 0–02–688504–2 (softcover)

Contents

The Rocky Earth

WHEREVER YOU'RE STANDING at this moment—even if it's on the deck of a ship far out at sea—there is rock underneath you. The entire outside of the earth is a shell of hard rock called the crust. A great deal of the crust is covered with water—the ocean—and where the crust sticks up above the water, as continents and islands, much of it is covered with soil and growing things. But everywhere beneath sea or soil, the crust is there, about 3 to 5 miles thick under the water and about 20 to 25 miles thick under the land.

Beneath the hard, cool crust lies a 1,800-mile-deep section of layers of rock, called the mantle, that is progressively hotter the deeper it reaches. Below it is a 1,400-mile-deep layer of seething hot, molten material, probably metal. And beneath this is the earth's inner core: a 1,600-mile-thick ball of incredibly hot material, also probably metal, that despite its heat is literally squeezed solid by the tremendous pressure pressing it together. Thus, the earth is a ball of mostly rock and metal.

The rocks in the earth's crust were formed in several ways. Some were once part of the mantle. Through volcanic action and other ways, molten rock was sometimes pushed up from the mantle into or onto the crust. There it cooled and hardened, becoming basalt, granite, or other types of rock called *igneous*, meaning "fiery."

Sometimes, rocks already in the crust sank toward the mantle, where they were changed by the tremendous heat and pressure. When they were pushed back up into the crust as part of a new mountain range, they formed what is called *metamorphic*, or changed, rock, such as slate and marble. Of course, this process took millions of years.

And many of earth's rocks were formed by a sort of squeezing-together process, in the sea. Billions of bits of rock were always being rubbed loose from the crust by the action of rains and the flowing water of streams and rivers. These rock bits were carried to the sea, where they sank to the bottom. There, they were slowly squeezed together as more and more of them piled atop one another, forming sandstone, limestone, and other types of rock known as *sedimentary*, or settled, rock. This process, too, took a long, long time.

The processes of making rocks go on today just as in the past. At this very

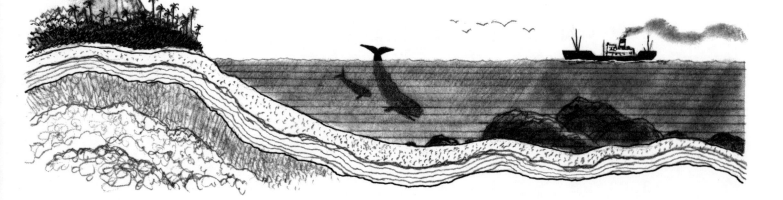

Crystal shapes can be seen with a microscope.

moment, igneous, metamorphic, and sedimentary rocks are still being formed.

Most of the rock that makes up the earth's hard crust isn't just one kind of material; it's often a mixture of solids, liquids, and even gases. Many kinds of rock are actually mixtures of *mixtures* of things.

The different kinds of materials that form rocks are what we call minerals. Minerals are the natural, solid, lifeless substances that make up most of the ball of the earth. The word *mineral* comes from the word *mine*, which, of course, means "a hole dug in the earth in order to take things out." However, not everything dug out of the earth is a mineral. Coal and oil, even though they come from beneath the crust, are not minerals, because they are formed from the substance of things that were once alive—plants and animals. A mineral is a substance that never lived.

Minerals, like everything else in the world—and in the whole universe, for that matter—are formed out of particles called atoms, which are so tiny it takes billions of them to form even a tiny grain of dust. There are more than a hundred different kinds of atoms, and each different kind is what we call an element—a *basic* substance. A good many minerals—such as gold, copper, and sulfur—are elements, formed of only one kind of atom.

Elements often combine with one another, and a substance formed out of two or more combined elements is called a *compound,* which simply means "mixture." Most minerals are compounds, and

a compound can be broken down, or taken apart, into the elements that form it. It's important to be able to break down compounds, because a lot of elements are locked up in compounds in certain minerals. The only way we can make use of these elements is by breaking down the compound, usually by heating it.

Most minerals, whether they're elements or compounds, have one thing in common. Their atoms, either all one kind or a mixture of several kinds, are packed together in a certain pattern, rather than just in any old jumble. Because of this, these minerals tend to have even, geometrical shapes with flat sides, such as cubes. These shapes are called crystals.

In many minerals, the crystal shapes can't be seen except with a powerful microscope. But other minerals are formed into large crystals that often look as if someone had carved or chiseled them. They are shaped like cubes, pyramids, diamonds, six-sided bars, bricks, books, boards, needles, and book pages. Crystals sometimes grow together to form tiny crosses, arrowheads, and other shapes that look as if they must have been artificially made. However, most crystals are never as perfect as if someone had really made them. They are usually quite lopsided and irregular.

Crystals form in several ways. Hot, molten rock or metal cooling and growing solid is one of these ways. The atoms, which move rapidly while they are hot, slow down and become locked into a pattern that gradually builds up. If the cool-

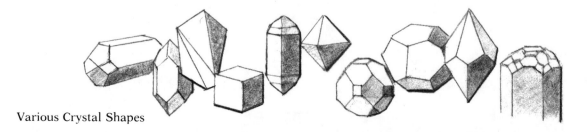

Various Crystal Shapes

A harder mineral will scratch
a softer one.

ing is very slow, the crystals that form are usually large.

A second way is by the sudden cooling of hot gas. Atoms of certain elements will then suddenly lock together, forming crystals that come showering down out of the gas like snowflakes falling from a cloud.

A third way crystals form is through the slow evaporation of liquid that has minerals dissolved in it. The atoms of the minerals are farther apart in liquid form, and as the liquid evaporates, these atoms move closer together, forming patterns and becoming hard crystals.

The way a mineral's atoms are packed together gives the mineral its particular shape and often affects how the mineral breaks. Atoms packed in a certain way don't hold together as tightly in some directions as they do in others, and this causes some minerals always to break into certain shapes. For example, the mineral galena, which is formed in cubic crystals, always breaks into cubes. The mineral mica always splits into thin sheets. Minerals that break cleanly in such a way are said to have "cleavage." Many minerals don't have cleavage; instead they "fracture." Flint, for example, fractures into curved chips that somewhat resemble half a clam shell. Some metals, such as silver and copper, will fracture into jagged pieces.

The way a mineral's atoms are packed also affects its hardness. When a crystal structure is built up of small atoms that are closely packed, that mineral will be harder than one in which the atoms are more loosely packed. Mineralogists, scientists who study minerals, check a mineral's hardness with a scratch test—a harder mineral will always scratch a softer one. A piece of calcite can be scratched with a piece of quartz, and the quartz can be scratched with a diamond, the hardest of all minerals.

Many minerals look much alike, but mineralogists have several ways of identifying minerals. The scratch test is one way. Another way is with a streak test. When a mineral is crushed into powder, the powder often has a completely different color from that of the uncrushed mineral. For example, hematite, which is black on the outside, crushes into a red powder. The best way to check the color of a mineral's powder is to rub the mineral across the rough surface of a piece of white porcelain called a streak plate. The mineral will leave a colored streak that helps the mineralogist identify it.

Minerals have always been tremendously important to humans. Many minerals, in the foods we eat, are used by our bodies and are actually essential in keeping us alive. Minerals were used for our first tools and weapons and to create our first works of art. They are still used for such purposes. Minerals have provided us with thousands of useful things that we have come to accept as part of our everyday life. Many people collect minerals and rocks just for fun; but the serious study of minerals is an important one that can help, and has helped, our civilization grow.

Quartz—Tools, Magic, and Electricity

THERE WAS A TIME, several million years ago, when the ancestors of human beings were nothing more than just rather smart, apelike animals. But these smart animals learned to do something no other animal could do—make stones into tools. And that use of minerals for tools helped put human beings on the path to civilization.

The first human tool was made simply by pounding one rock with another. This knocked chips off the stone being pounded, giving it some jagged, sharp edges that could be used for hacking hunks of meat off dead animals. During hundreds of thousands of years, humans learned how to chip a chunk of stone into a sharp-edged ax and then learned how to shape chips of stone into knives, spearheads, drills, scrapers, and other useful tools. This long period of time when people made all their tools and weapons out of stone is now called the Stone Age.

But the stone that Stone Age people used for making things wasn't just any old stone. It had to be a glassy sort of stone that would chip easily, leaving sharp edges. One such stone is flint, a dark gray, brownish, or black mineral found in lumps in chalk rocks and limestone. Flint is a compound of the solid element called silicon and the gas element oxygen, and this compound, known as silica, is one of the main ingredients in glass. A person who knew how could press a chunk of flint with a bone or a piece of wood and make a long, slim, flat chip break off. Then by breaking tiny chips from the long chip, the toolmaker could form a sharp-edged, pointed knife or spearhead that had a rather glassy look and edges so thin that light passed through them.

Flint also was useful to prehistoric peoples in another way. If a piece of flint and a chunk of iron are struck together, they generally produce a shower of sparks. Sparks are hot, of course, and if they fall upon something very dry, they'll often start a fire. When people of long ago discovered this, they began using flint and iron to start fires, which was much quicker than twirling one stick of wood against another. For thousands of years, until the invention of matches, people used flint and steel to start fires. Modern cigarette lighters still use this principle, but the "flint" in a cigarette lighter isn't really flint anymore. It's a mixture of iron and a metal called cerium, which works like flint but can be molded into thin rods.

12

Striking flint and iron produces sparks.

SMOKY QUARTZ

ROSE QUARTZ

CHALCEDONY
(Chrysoprase)

CITRINE

AMETHYST

AGATE

Although it appears to be quite different, flint is actually a form of the mineral quartz, which generally looks like chunks of broken glass with six sides and pointed ends. It is often called rock crystal. Pure rock crystal is much like glass, colorless and transparent, but if other substances are mixed into it, it becomes colored. There's a brown or black quartz called smoky quartz, and a reddish quartz called rose quartz. Yellow quartz is called citrine, and purple quartz is called amethyst. Amethyst is the birthstone for people born in February, and it's a semiprecious stone, often used as a jewel in rings and necklaces.

To many primitive peoples, the transparent, shiny crystals of quartz seemed like a kind of dry, frozen water, so they often used the crystals for "water magic." Some of the Australian aborigine people used quartz in a magical ceremony to make rain fall. They broke crystals of quartz into tiny bits that looked like raindrops, then poured showers of these "raindrops" over one another, in hopes this would trick real rain into falling.

Actually, quartz does have a special "power," and it's a power that has been extremely useful to the civilized world. Quartz possesses what is known as piezoelectric effect. That simply means that if a piece of quartz is squeezed in a vice, it produces electricity. And if such a piece of quartz is connected to a source of alternating electrical current, the quartz can be made to vibrate, or squeeze in and out, millions of times a second. So, quartz crystals are used in devices called oscillators, which are used by radio and television transmitters to change vibrations into radio waves. Pieces of specially cut quartz are also used in microphones, telephone receivers, radios, and hearing aids. Thus, quartz plays a very important role in modern communications.

A form of quartz called chalcedony is usually found in lumpy clusters, like bunches of grapes pushed together. These clusters occur in cracks and crevices in rocky places where the chalcedony was formed by silica—a mixture of silicon and oxygen—carried there a little at a time by trickling water and left behind when the water evaporated. Chalcedony is usually a smoky blue color but may also be white, gray, brown, red, yellow, green, or colorless. Red chalcedony is called carnelian and is sometimes used as a jewel. People all over the world have ascribed magical powers to it. It was believed to give courage in battle, protect against evil sorcery, drive off evil spirits—and keep teeth from falling out! Another form of chalcedony is green with reddish flecks that look like splotches of blood, and it is often called bloodstone.

Still another form of chalcedony is agate, which is streaked with many colors in bands, stripes, and swirls. Agate is often found inside round pieces of stone called geodes. Saw a geode in half and you'll generally find it lined with beautiful bands of colored crystals. A geode starts to form when a small dead animal or plant that's buried in mud decays, leav-

14

ing a "pocket" inside the mud. The pocket then fills up with water. Over a great many years the mud begins to harden into rock with the pocket of water still inside, and a thin shell of silica forms around the water. In time, crystals of chalcedony from minerals in the water form all around the inside of the shell. Sometimes, a geode can be found that still has water in it.

Agate and chalcedony are the main substances that form the tree trunks of the famous Petrified Forest in northern Arizona. About 150 million years ago, these trunks were live, growing trees, and the desert in which they now lie was a dense, green forest where dinosaurs roamed. As the trees died, they fell to the ground and slowly sank into the mud. The wood began to rot, and water filled with miner-

als—mostly silica—seeped into it. As the water evaporated, the silica was left behind, forming stone. In time, all the wood in the trunks was replaced by stone, in most cases agate and chalcedony. Today, the stone trunks lie in the Painted Desert of Arizona.

Agate, with its pretty, swirling colors, has been well known to children for a good many years, for it has always been used to make the very best kind of marbles for the game of marbles. A marble made of real agate is called an aggie.

So, as you can see, the mineral quartz in all its forms has certainly given people a great many things—everything from the material for our first tools and weapons, to a material that helps radios and television sets work, to the aggie that's the best marble in the bag!

Copper — The First Tool Metal

A MAN SAT IN THE SHADE of a rocky cliff wall, examining an object he held in his hand. It was a ragged, lumpy chunk of dull brown rock, shaped much like a tree branch. He had found the rock that morning while crossing a ravine. Its odd shape had caught his eye, and he had picked it up.

The man was a skilled flintworker, and he wondered if this strange rock could be chipped like flint. Putting it on the ground, he picked up the heavy, round, tennis-ball-sized piece of stone he used as a hammer and tapped the rock with it, sharply. He struck several more times, each harder, but the rock did not chip or split.

To test the rock's strength, the man began to pound it steadily, striking with all his might. It was strong; no matter how hard or often he struck it, it did not break. And yet—the man picked up the rock and peered closely at it with growing interest—his pounding *had* done something. The spot he had been hitting with the hammer had flattened out and grown smooth and shiny, with a bright orange color! Although the rock was so hard it wouldn't break, it was yet somehow so soft that pounding could change its shape, as well as make it bright and colorful. The man grew more and more excited as he realized that by steadily hammering this odd piece of stone, he might make it into something.

The rock the flintworker had found wasn't actually a rock, of course. It was a chunk of the shiny orange metal we now call copper, from which most electrical wire for light and power is made. Today, most copper is dug out of the earth and is mixed with other minerals. But in prehistoric times, lumps of pure, or native, copper could often be found lying right on the ground in dry riverbeds and rocky places. Prehistoric peoples sometimes picked up these chunks and in time learned that copper could be pounded into shapes and even into thin sheets. No one now knows exactly when this discovery was made, but a piece of a necklace more than 11,000 years old, made of hammered copper, has been found in Iraq.

At first, because of its shine and pretty color, copper was probably used mostly for making beads and bracelets. But before long people realized it could also be hammered to form such things as knife

16

CHALCOPYRITE

BANDED MALACHITE

CUPRITE

NATIVE COPPER

blades, spearheads, and chisels. This was an important discovery, for copper was a much better material than flint for making tools and weapons. Flint often broke while being hammered or used as a tool, but copper wouldn't break, split, or chip.

About 5,000 years ago, still another great discovery was made. People somewhere in the Near East learned that the chunks of pure copper they'd been picking up off the ground were not the only form of copper. They found that when certain kinds of rocks were heated in a good, hot fire, a shimmering orange liquid would flow out of them, and when this liquid cooled, it was copper! These people had discovered what we now call ores—minerals that contain metals (and usually other things) which can be removed from them by means of heat. This is the process known as smelting.

Knowledge of how to smelt copper ores spread through the Near East and, after a time, throughout most of the ancient world. One of the first copper ores people learned to use was the green, bumpy rock we call malachite. Oddly enough, even though malachite contains copper, which prehistoric peoples couldn't break no matter how hard they tried, malachite itself can be broken and can even be ground into a powder. Ancient peoples in the Near East broke chunks of malachite out of rocks in the desert, pounded them into tiny pieces, and poured the pieces onto hot coals in a pit. Liquid copper would flow out of the pieces, leaving behind a rough ash, or slag, and trickle down to the bottom of the pit. After the coals had burned up and the ashes had cooled, the lumps of copper at the bottom of the pit were gathered.

Probably by trial and error, ancient peoples found many other ores of copper, such as the bright red mineral cuprite, which often looks like chunks of red glass, and the soft, golden-yellow mineral chalcopyrite. Today, we know of about 165 different minerals that contain copper.

Once people had learned that hot, liquid copper that came out of ores cooled into hard metal, they quickly got the idea of making molds for spear and ax heads and other things and pouring the liquid metal into the molds. No longer did they have to hammer the copper into shape; now they simply let the hot metal cool into the shape they wanted. Five thousand years ago, the soldiers of Sumer and other ancient lands of the Near East carried spears tipped with points of copper that had been molded in this way.

Copper was humankind's first metal used for tools, and it took us out of the Stone Age. Today, it is probably even more important to us than it was in prehistoric times, for it is one of the best and cheapest conductors, or carriers, of electricity. Most copper used today comes from the ores bornite, chalcopyrite, chalcocite, cuprite, malachite, and azurite, which are dug out of other rocks. There are very few chunks of pure copper, such as prehistoric peoples were able to find, now left.

Copper wires conduct electricity.

Cassiterite — Tin and Bronze

SOME 2,500 YEARS AGO, on the plain of Marathon, the warriors of the Greek cities of Athens and Plataea were preparing to defend their land against the invading army of the mighty Persian Empire.

The sun sparkled on the armor and weapons of the Greek soldiers. Spearheads winked with a yellow gleam, and armor shone with a golden glimmer. To anyone looking at them, the Greeks would have seemed to be wearing armor of gold. It wasn't gold, of course—but the metal we call bronze, and the Greeks at Marathon lived during the Bronze Age.

Bronze is a metal that, when new and polished, shines like gold. It isn't a natural substance, like copper; it's an artificial combination of two minerals. Soon after people learned to smelt and cast copper, they found that mixing copper with another substance made it harder, for better weapons and tools. This was bronze.

The first bronze was a mixture of copper and the gray, flaky mineral arsenic. This probably came about by chance, because some of the copper ore that was smelted had arsenic in it. But seeing that this metal was tougher than plain copper, people must have figured out that something was mixed with the copper and experimented until they found what it was. Then they probably mixed arsenic with copper on purpose.

But there's one trouble with arsenic—it's poisonous! Workers who breathed the fumes of heated arsenic must have gotten sick, in time, and some might have died. People soon realized they couldn't use arsenic for making bronze.

They probably tried a number of other things until they came to tin. Tin is a bright, silvery, rather soft metal, and its main source is a hard, heavy mineral ore called cassiterite. Cassiterite is usually formed as dark reddish-brown, black, or yellow stubby, four- or eight-sided, pointed crystals. However, chunks of cassiterite, rounded and smoothed by long journeys down the mountains, can often be found in streams. Some metalsmiths of long ago must have tried smelting some of these pebbles and found they produced metal. When the smiths tried mixing some of the metal with copper, the result was fine bronze.

We still get most of our tin from cassiterite and still mix it with copper to make bronze. But tin is also used in a number of other things—such as tin cans. Actually, a tin can is made from a thin sheet of steel that's just coated on both sides with a very light covering of tin. The tin is used because it's rust resistant.

A lot of things that you often use, such as safety pins and paper clips, are also made of steel coated with tin. Tin is mixed with lead to make solder, and tin is also mixed with tiny amounts of copper and a bluish-white, brittle metal called antimony to make pewter.

19

Gold — The Most Precious Metal

WHILE HIS ASSISTANT STOKED the fire in the brick oven, the alchemist carefully stirred the mixture in the heavy pot. His eyes gleamed hopefully as he peered at the substance which would soon be boiling and smoking over the fire. This time, he was sure he had it—this time, he was sure he would make gold!

Gold! For thousands of years people have braved dangers to search for it, have fought for it, have even murdered for it! During ancient and medieval times, the men known as alchemists even tried to make gold artificially, out of mixtures of various things. They never succeeded, of course, but they learned a lot about minerals, elements, and compounds, and their discoveries were the beginning of our science of chemistry.

Gold may well have been the very first metal to be used by people, for prehistoric peoples probably used it for ornaments before they used copper for tools. They must have seen nuggets of gold gleaming up from river bottoms and streambeds and picked them up because of their pretty shine and color. Such nuggets came from up in the mountains, where veins of gold ran, like crooked branches, through masses of quartz and other rocks. When mountain snows melted in the springtime, rushing water poured down the mountainside, tearing away bits of the gold and carrying them into streams and rivers. In time, chunks of gold came to rest beneath the water, wedged among rocks and partly buried in sand. Most of these chunks became smooth and rounded from constant rubbing against harder rocks and sand. It's not possible to say exactly when people started picking up such gold nuggets for use as ornaments, but nuggets have been found in ancient graves of Stone Age people.

Gold always stays beautiful. It won't rust as iron will or tarnish like silver or turn dull like copper. It is soft enough to be hammered into sheets as thin as tissue paper—the thinnest sheets of *any* metal—and ancient peoples found that such sheets could be rubbed onto pottery and wooden objects to make them gleam with golden beauty. Gold can be easily formed into thin wire and can be melted and cast into any shape. People must have begun long ago to make it into jewelry and ornaments. In ancient Egypt and Iraq, gold was being made into beautiful objects more than 5,000 years ago.

But gold was not only more beautiful to ancient peoples than was copper or iron or most metals, it was also harder to find than most of them. So it quickly became a precious material that could belong only to wealthy people or nobles and that was used for making idols and other religious objects. And because it was precious and sacred, many legends grew up about it.

Panning for Gold

20

PYRITE
(Fool's Gold)

GOLD VEIN
IN QUARTZ

CHALCOPYRITE

GOLD NUGGETS

Gold was once used to treat the sick.

People believed it was formed by the sun and that it was the most perfect of all things. People even came to believe it was a medicine that could cure anything. In China, it was mixed into a salve and rubbed on the bodies of sick people, and in Europe, it was sometimes made into a drink for the sick!

Gold is still the world's most precious metal. It's now used not only for jewelry and ornaments, but also for money by all the world's nations. Most countries do not make gold coins, but they keep supplies of gold bars to pay for things purchased from other nations.

Because gold is so soft, when it is made into jewelry it usually has to be mixed with another metal, such as copper or silver, to make it hard enough to keep from getting scratched, bent, or dented. The amount of gold in a piece of jewelry is measured in "karats." A karat is one twenty-fourth part of a whole amount, so something that is "14 karat gold" is 14 parts gold and 10 parts something else. Of course, "24 karat gold"—twenty-four twenty-fourths—is pure gold.

Much of the world's gold comes from mines where veins of gold run through masses of quartz. People searching for gold among quartz and other rocks have often been fooled by other minerals that have a yellowish shine. Three minerals in particular—pyrite, chalcopyrite, and vermiculite—have fooled so many people they've become known as fool's gold. But there are several ways to tell whether a yellowish mineral is real gold or fool's gold. Probably the easiest way is just to pound it with a hammer. Soft real gold will start to flatten out, but all the kinds of fool's gold will usually just break.

Silver—The Moon's Metal

HOW DO YOU KILL a werewolf? With a silver bullet, of course!

The element silver, a metal, has almost always been thought to have great power over evil things. Perhaps this is because silver was once thought to be associated with the moon, and moonlight drives away night's blackness in which evil creatures lurk and prowl. At any rate, people throughout Europe once believed that a werewolf, wicked sorcerer, witch, or other evil creature with a charmed life could be killed only with a silver weapon. In China, wealthy people often wore lockets of silver that were supposed to protect them from evil. In parts of France, people on their way to be married at church were wrapped together with a silver chain so they couldn't be bewitched on the way!

Silver is a bendable metal, so soft it can

22

be scratched with the blade of a knife. When polished, it's a beautiful silvery white, but it tarnishes very quickly, turning a muddy, dark gray. Pieces of silver that look like bunches of twisted wire or clusters of stubby branches are sometimes found among rocks. However, most native, or unmixed, silver is found in masses and slabs that are sometimes enormous. A piece of silver found in a mine in Canada was nearly 100 feet long and 60 feet thick and was known as the silver sidewalk!

But silver is most often found locked into a number of different minerals, such as argentite and cerargyrite. People in the Near East were smelting silver from such ores as much as 5,000 years ago. Today, most silver actually comes as a by-product from galena, an ore of lead. When the galena is smelted for lead, some silver is usually recovered, too.

Silver was always regarded as the second-most-precious metal after gold— some people regarded it as even more precious than gold—so it was generally used only for making jewelry and works of art. Today, silver is still used mostly for jewelry and for things that are both pretty and useful, such as teapots. However, it's also now used in other ways. Silver is compounded with various things to make substances called silver nitrate and silver bromide, which are used in the manufacture of photographic film. Silver nitrate is also used as a medicine, to treat several eye and skin diseases.

You may have heard the term *sterling silver* used for silverware. That simply means that each piece of the silverware is made of at least 92 percent silver. The word *sterling* apparently comes from an old name for a pure silver coin.

Sulfur — The Burning Stone

THE NAME *sulfur* is an old, old one. It's from the Latin word for "burning stone." Thousands of years ago, people knew that chunks of sulfur, which looked to them like yellowish, glassy rocks, would burn with an eerie blue flame and a strong smell. In those days, people got all their sulfur from the ground around the mouths of rumbling, smoking volcanoes or from the edges of bubbling, smelly hot springs. Because of this, they had the idea that sulfur was associated with heat, smoke, steam, volcanic eruptions, and rumblings deep in the earth. In time, people in Europe came to believe that such things had something to do with the devil. They called sulfur *brimstone*, which also means "burning stone," and they were sure that hell was a place of fire and brimstone!

Because of its strong smell, people of ancient and medieval times used burning sulfur to purify and fumigate their homes, temples, and churches, driving off insects, rats, and other pests. Sulfur also was one of the minerals most widely used by alchemists, who tried all sorts of things with it. These experiments with sulfur resulted in the invention of gunpowder, which is a mixture of sulfur, powdered charcoal, and a mineral called saltpeter.

No one knows who invented gunpowder, but it was probably invented somewhere in southern Europe about 700 years ago, by someone who was trying different things in combination with sulfur.

Sulfur is a brittle yellow mineral usually found in clumps of four- and six-sided crystals and sometimes in clusters of needle-shaped crystals. The crystals of pure sulfur found around volcanoes were "chilled" out of the hot gases that poured from the volcanoes, in the same way that snowflakes (which are also crystals) are chilled out of clouds of water vapor on a cold day. Sulfur is also found down in the earth, mixed with huge masses of limestone and gypsum, especially those that form caps on enormous domes of salt. And sulfur is often found combined with metals to form ores, such as galena, the ore of lead; cinnabar, the ore of mercury; argentite, an ore of silver; and several others. Compounds of sulfur and other minerals are known as sulfides.

Sulfur is an important mineral needed by living things. It performs special duties in the bodies of people and animals, such as helping change food into energy and helping bones grow. We get most of the sulfur our bodies need from foods such as

SULFUR CRYSTALS
Sicily

SULFUR CRYSTALS
Yellowstone Park

Crop Dusting With a Pesticide
Containing Sulfur

eggs, onions, and cabbage.

Sulfur has a great many uses. It's still used for making gunpowder, and it's one of the chemicals mixed together to make the heads of matches. It's used in making fertilizers that help farm crops grow and pesticides that kill weeds and insects that damage crops. It's an important ingredient in a number of medicines and an important part of the processes for refining rubber and making artificial rubber.

When sulfur is burned, it gives off sulfur dioxide gas, which when mixed with steam, forms a liquid called sulfuric acid. And sulfuric acid is used for an amazing number of things—purifying gasoline, making laundry soaps, paper, steel, and even dynamite and nitroglycerin. Sulfuric acid is also used in automobile batteries.

Altogether, the list of things for which we use the element sulfur is nearly endless! Fortunately, sulfur is plentiful.

Hematite — Paint and Iron

IN CAVES and on smooth rock walls of cliffs, in many parts of the world, there are paintings made tens of thousands of years ago by prehistoric peoples. Some of these paintings are pictures of animals—running horses, lumbering bison, and other creatures that prehistoric peoples hunted for food. Other paintings are simply designs or strange shapes, the meanings of which we can now only guess.

One of the main colors in many of these paintings is a rich, brownish red. Another color often present is a brownish yellow. Both colors were made from minerals that the people of tens of thousands of years ago had learned to grind to a powder and mix with animal fat to make paint.

The reddish stuff the red paint was made from is now called red ocher, and

it's still used for making paint. Red ocher is a form of the mineral hematite, which usually looks like black, lumpy rock. But even though it's black, when it is rubbed against the rough surface of a streak plate, it leaves a dark red mark the color of red ocher. Because this redness resembles dried blood, the mineral was given its name—*hematite* means "bloodlike."

The substance used for making the yellow paint is now called yellow ocher, and it, too, is still used for making paint. Yellow ocher is a form of a brownish mineral called goethite, which leaves a brownish-yellow streak on a streak plate.

Hematite and goethite are very important minerals, far more important than just for making paint. They're two of the main minerals from which we get the

26

metal iron. People didn't find out about iron until after they had been making things out of copper and bronze for quite a while. But by about 3,400 years ago, people somewhere in the Near East had discovered that when chunks of hematite or goethite or one of the other ores of iron were heated in a hot enough fire, they gave off a dark, shimmery liquid that cooled into dull-black metal. This metal wasn't really any harder than bronze, but when people learned how to heat the metal with charcoal and cool it suddenly by plunging it into water, they found that it became much harder and tougher than any other metal then known. It made better swords, arrowheads, plows, and sickles than did bronze, which quickly lost its sharpness and was easily bent. The discovery of how to harden iron ended the Bronze Age and began the Iron Age.

People who first possessed weapons and armor of iron were easily able to conquer those who still had only bronze or stone weapons. Iron was so important in ancient warfare that when the Etruscans conquered the Romans, more than 2,400 years ago, they forbade the Romans to make any weapons of iron! To ancient peoples, iron seemed almost a magical substance, with great power. In time, people even came to believe that iron had power over supernatural creatures. Many old, old legends and myths from all over the world tell how demons, ogres, wicked fairies, and other evil, supernatural beings were driven off or destroyed by an iron weapon, tool, or even a necklace or charm made of iron.

Men who knew how to work iron and turn it into weapons and tools were very important members of their tribe or community. Because these men beat the hot metal with hammers to give it strength and shape, they were usually called by a word that meant "beater" in whatever language their people spoke. Such a word is the Old English word *smith*. So is the German word *schmit*. In time, such words became the ironworkers' names. Today, people named Smith, Schmitt, Ferrar, Herrera, Kovacs, Kowalski, Gowan, MacGowan, or McGowen probably had an ancestor who worked with iron.

Iron is just as important now as it was long ago. Much of it is made into steel, without which our civilization could hardly exist!

Iron Charm

Blacksmiths Working With Iron

Calcite — Buildings and Statues

YOU HAVE PROBABLY often seen the kind of rock called marble. It's usually very pretty—smooth and glossy and swirling with pale colors like frozen smoke. Marble is used on the floors, walls, and ceilings of many large buildings.

You've probably often seen the rock called limestone, too, for it's also used in many buildings. Limestone isn't as pretty as marble, though. It's white, gray, or yellowish, and rather rough looking.

Yet, all smooth, beautiful marble was once drab, rough limestone! Marble is limestone that was changed by the forces of the earth.

Limestone is made up mostly of crystals of the mineral calcite, which is a compound of calcium, oxygen, and carbon. (When not mixed with other materials, calcium atoms form a rather soft, whitish metal; oxygen is a colorless gas; and carbon is usually the sooty stuff left over when something burns.) Limestone is sedimentary rock, formed in water. Some limestone was formed from calcite that was dissolved in seawater. As water was evaporated by sunlight, solid calcite crystals were formed and drifted to the sea bottom. Over many years, they piled up and formed a thick ooze that, in much more time, hardened into limestone.

However, most limestone was actually formed out of seashells—the shells, or "outside skeletons," of billions and billions of sea creatures, such as snails, and coral polyps. These creatures grow their shells much as humans grow bones. Their bodies take calcium and carbon out of the food they eat and mix them together to make calcite, the hard substance that forms their shells. When the creatures die, their soft bodies decay, leaving only the hard shell. Over an enormous amount of time, billions and billions of shells, crushed to bits and squeezed together, form layers of limestone.

And during earth's hundreds of millions of years of existence, many layers of limestone turned into marble. This happened in two ways. One way was by the surging of seething hot, molten rock from the mantle up into the crust where there was limestone. The tremendous shock of heat changed the limestone to marble. The other way was through the sinking of layers of limestone into the depths of the crust during the titanic, ages-long process that forms mountains. There, subjected to tremendous heat and pressure, the limestone changed. In time, as new mountain

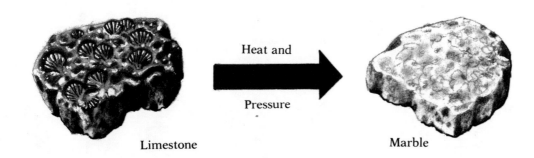

Limestone   Heat and Pressure   Marble

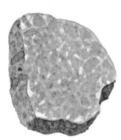

MARBLE

CALCITE

DOLOMITE

SHELL LIMESTONE

ranges were pushed up out of the earth, these huge masses of changed limestone—now marble—were thrust up as parts of the mountains.

Marble is still calcite, but the crystals are squeezed together much more tightly than they are in limestone. Thus, marble is much *denser* and has no cavities, or "pores," so it can be polished to a smooth, lustrous gloss.

If the calcite in marble is pure, with nothing mixed into it, the marble is perfectly white. Pure white marble is known as statuary marble, for throughout history, the world's greatest sculptors have preferred using this kind of marble to make their greatest works of art.

But most often other minerals are combined with the calcite, and then the marble may be pinkish or streaked with pale green or swirls of gray. For thousands of years, such colored marbles have been used for beautifying buildings.

Some limestone and marble is formed of the mineral dolomite instead of calcite. Dolomite is a compound of calcium, oxygen, carbon, and a grayish-white metal called magnesium. Both calcite and dolomite are also found as crystals growing on other kinds of rock. Calcite crystals are most often shaped like lopsided cubes. Dolomite crystals are of the same shape, but the sides are sometimes slightly curved.

Halite—A Mineral We Eat Every Day

ONE OF THE MOST important foods we eat every day is a mineral. Common table salt is a mineral that has the official name *halite*. It is a compound of sodium and chlorine, which separated out into their "true" forms—that is, with their atoms not combined with anything else—would be a soft, silvery-white metal and a *poisonous* yellowish-green gas!

Most of the salt bought in stores comes from the earth, dug out of vast, gleaming salt mines or pumped out of the ground by a special process. This salt was left behind by the evaporation of ancient seas, for an enormous amount of salt is dissolved in seawater. In some parts of the world, people "harvest" sea salt, simply by letting trays of seawater evaporate.

Salt, whether from the ground or the sea, always has the form of a cube-shaped crystal, and no matter how finely the crystals may be ground up, they will always break into smaller cubes. You can grow halite crystals and at the same time see how salt is left behind by evaporation. Mix a teaspoonful of salt into about six teaspoonfuls of water. Stir thoroughly until the salt is dissolved—the water will

Salt is harvested from the sea.

turn from cloudy to almost clear. Pour the water into a shallow pan or saucer, and leave it in a warm, dry place for a day or so. When all the water has evaporated, you'll see fairly large white cubes clustered at the bottom of the saucer. If you own a microscope, crush the cubes to powder by grinding them with the back of a spoon, and look at some of the powder through your microscope. You'll see that it's made up of tiny, tiny cubes!

Salt is an extremely important substance for nearly all living things. It does a number of vital jobs in our bodies, and we actually couldn't live if we didn't always have a certain amount of salt inside us! On the other hand, too much salt can be bad for people—it can damage the organ called a kidney, and many doctors think it causes a disease called high blood pressure.

Salt was one of the most important trade goods of the ancient world, and some of the very first roads were simply trails made by salt traders as they carried their salt to communities that hungered for it. The ancient Romans even built a special, fine long road just to carry salt from a distant mine to the city of Rome. The Roman soldiers received part of their pay in salt, and this payment was known as a *salarium*, which means "salt money." Our word *salary* comes from this word. A soldier who shirked his duty was contemptuously said to be "not worth his salt," an expression we still use for someone who doesn't do the job he's paid to do.

Because of its importance, salt became a symbol *of* importance. In medieval times, at meals served in the great castles and palaces, a large container of salt, called a *saler*, was placed in the middle of the long dining table. The highest noble present sat at the head of the table. All the most important people sat at the half of the table closest to the noble and were said to be "above the salt." The less important people sat "below the salt."

Even though salt is such an important food for people, only a tiny, tiny amount of all the salt taken from the ground and the sea is used for food. Much salt is used in the manufacture of paper, soap, leather goods, glass, and many other things. And one of its most important uses in many places is to melt snow and ice to keep roads and railroad tracks clear in the winter. It's certainly one of the most useful minerals that Mother Earth gives us!

Salt Lick

Jade—Works of Art and Butcher Knives

Jade Pendant
China, 400 B.C.

THE BEAUTIFUL GREEN or white stone known as jade has been used for thousands of years to make marvelous works of art. But it was once also used for making butcher knives to cut up "meat" for cannibal feasts!

The stone called jade is actually two different kinds of stone: the minerals nephrite and jadeite. Nephrite is a compound of silica; water; iron; magnesium, a light metal; and calcium. Jadeite is a compound of silica, aluminum, and sodium, one of the elements that forms table salt. Nephrite, which is usually green or white and is the more common of the two minerals, was more often used by people for thousands of years and was first called by the name *jade*. Jadeite, which is much less common, has a cloudy, emerald-green form known as imperial jade, but jadeite may also be white, yellow, pale purple, or dark red.

Both these minerals have needlelike crystals that form a tightly woven locked-together structure that makes the stones extremely hard to break but easy to carve. This made jade ideal for early tools and weapons, and prehistoric peoples in parts of the world where nephrite was available made it into axes and spearheads. And it

was on New Caledonia—an island in the Pacific Ocean where, until about a hundred years ago, many of the primitive people practiced cannibalism—that knives made of jade were used for cutting up human flesh to be cooked and eaten!

But the main use of jade, especially the green and white kinds, was for finely carved jewelry, ornaments, and art objects, and for thousands of years the finest carvers of jade have been the Chinese, to whom jade is known as *yu*. In old China, people believed that jade was actually pure water that had come from the highest mountains and had somehow become solid. For them it was the most precious of all minerals—even more precious than gold or any jewel. Chinese artists carved jade into beautiful vases, boxes, bowls and dishes, little statues, and exquisitely intricate beads for necklaces. The Chinese also made jade into gongs, for when a thin piece of jade is gently tapped, it gives off a deep, long-lasting, very pleasing tone.

Jade was also highly prized by the ancient Aztec people of Mexico, where it was very rare. Aztec artists carved the stone into statues of their gods, and Aztec nobles wore jade ornaments in their ears, noses, and lips!

Jade Statues
Aztec

JADEITE

NEPHRITE

JADEITE

WHITE JADEITE

YELLOW JADEITE

Galena—Type, Bullets, and Radiation Shields

GALENA IS A MINERAL that's usually found as clusters of hard, shiny, bluish-gray cubes embedded in limestone or other rock. A compound of sulfur and the soft, silvery-gray metal lead, galena is the main ore from which lead is smelted. People found out how to get lead from galena long ago, in prehistoric times. It was too soft to use for tools or weapons—you can even scratch it with your fingernail—so people used it for making ornaments, weights for scales, and coins.

Lead is easy to melt and easy to mold into shapes. The ancient Romans must have liked the way molded, polished lead looked, because they made cups and dishes out of it. Actually, this was a dangerous thing, because in eating from lead plates, many Romans probably swallowed small amounts of lead with their food, and lead taken internally is poisonous. A lot of Romans may have died of lead poisoning, all because it was fashionable to have molded-lead plates!

During the Middle Ages, people somehow got the idea that lead could ward off demons and evil spirits, so precious objects and religious relics were often kept in chests and boxes made of lead. Many wealthy people even had themselves buried in lead coffins. Today, we know that lead really does keep out something "evil"—the deadly radiation given off by radioactive substances. Dangerous radioactive materials are kept in lead containers, and walls of lead are used to keep radiation from leaking out of nuclear power plants.

Lead played an important part in one of the world's greatest inventions. More than 500 years ago, someone—probably a German goldsmith named Johannes Gutenberg—got the idea of making a mold for each letter of the alphabet. From each mold, hundreds of metal letters could be cast, put together to make words, smeared with ink, and pressed against paper to make book pages. Thus, those molds, which were made of lead, made fast printing possible.

Lead is used for a great many things. There's lead in every battery, lead in many kinds of paint, and lead in some kinds of gasoline to keep car engines from "knocking." Lead is mixed with tin to make solder and is used to cover underground electrical cables to protect them from moisture. And of course, for hundreds of years, bullets have usually been made out of lead.

Graphite — The "Lead" That Isn't

WHEN YOU WRITE with a "lead" pencil, you're not really writing with lead at all. The dark marks are made by a mineral called graphite.

Graphite is a soft, smooth, slippery-feeling substance mostly found in large lumps or flattish, six-sided flakes in rocks. It splits easily into thin sheets and can also be easily crushed into powder. It is often called black lead, because when people first began writing with it, they thought it was a kind of lead. That's why, to this day, we still speak of "lead" pencils. It wasn't until 1789 that graphite was given its name, which comes from a Greek word that means "to write."

People first began using sticks of graphite as writing tools in England in the 1500's. That probably caused a lot of dirty fingers, however, and in the 1600's, a German inventor thought of putting a stick of graphite inside a piece of wood. More than 100 years later, in 1795, a Frenchman invented the way of making pencils that's still used today. Powdered graphite is mixed with clay and water to form a paste that's squeezed out into long strings by machines. The strings are cut to pencil-sized lengths and baked in ovens until hard. Each length is then fitted into a groove in a piece of wood that's a half-pencil. Another wooden half-pencil is glued to the first, and—presto—a "lead" pencil. If a lot of clay is mixed with the graphite, the lead will be harder and will make a light mark. Less clay will produce softer lead that makes a dark mark.

Graphite is used for a good many other things, too. It can take a lot of heat without melting, so it's used for making pots called crucibles, in which metals and other things can be melted. Electricity can be sent through graphite without making it burn and crumble as many metals do, so graphite is also used for making electrodes, which might be called the "doorways" through which electricity is sent into things. And because it is slick and slippery without being gummy like grease, graphite powder is used to lubricate locks and clocks, which have small parts grease could clog up.

Graphite is actually a native, or natural, form of the element carbon—carbon atoms lined up to form sheets that can slide against one another. It is one of the two mineral forms of carbon, and although it is soft and easily broken, the other form is the hardest substance known—diamond.

Present-Day Crucible

Graphite sticks were used before the invention of pencils.

Parts of space vehicles
are made of beryl.

Beryl — The Emerald

IN THE YEAR 1594, a Spanish horseman was riding through rocky countryside in the land known as the Spanish Main, which would one day be the nation of Colombia, South America. The rider noticed his horse had begun to limp, and suspected a pebble had gotten stuck in its hoof. Dismounting, he examined his steed's foot. Sure enough, there was a stone in the hoof—but the "stone" was a transparent, grass-green, six-sided crystal that the man recognized at once as an emerald!

Wild with excitement, the Spaniard turned and rode back the way he had come, gazing about sharp-eyed. And after searching for a time he found a mine that had been hidden by the Indians from the Spaniards who had conquered their land. That mine became the world's richest source of emeralds.

An emerald is the rarest and most valuable of all jewels. It is a form of beryl—an ore of a hard, light, gray-white metal called beryllium—which is used in making X-ray tubes, delicate instruments for aircraft, and parts of space vehicles. An ordinary crystal of beryl is a compound of beryllium, silicon, oxygen, and aluminum; and such crystals, which are smelted to get the metal from them, are usually a yellowish-green color. Sometimes, however, a tiny bit of chromium—which by itself is the metal used for making automobile bumpers and handles bright and shiny—is mixed in with the other things in a crystal of beryl. Then the beryl becomes a valuable, grass-green emerald.

In ancient times, many people believed that emeralds came from the nests of griffins, imaginary creatures that had the body of a lion with the head and wings of an eagle, said to live on high mountains in India. In medieval times, it was thought that emeralds had the power to cure fevers and prevent diseases such as leprosy and the dreadful sickness known as plague. It was said that anyone who carried an emerald would be smarter, have a better memory, be able to speak well, and would have health, wealth, strength, and happiness.

Crystals of beryl can also have other colors, caused by other substances mixed into them. A blue-green crystal is the gemstone called an aquamarine; yellow is called gold beryl; pink is morganite.

Emerald is the birthstone of people born in May.

36

Ancient Griffin

COMMON BERYL

EMERALD

AQUAMARINE

GOLD BERYL

MORGANITE

Cinnabar — "Live" Silver

THOUSANDS OF YEARS AGO, people knew that if they heated certain kinds of "rocks"—ores—a shiny liquid would flow out of them, and when the liquid cooled, it would become a hard metal. But, about 2,300 years ago, someone must have had a tremendous surprise when he heated a chunk of the sparkling, reddish rock we call cinnabar, which is most often found near volcanoes and hot springs. He got a shiny, silvery liquid out of it, all right, but when he waited for the liquid to harden, it *didn't*. This surprising substance stayed a liquid even after it was completely cool! He had discovered mercury, a metal whose natural form is liquid.

Mercury is such fascinating stuff that it would be tempting to play with it. Nobody should, for it is extremely poisonous! But someone who works with mercury—a chemist, for example—knows that although it's a liquid, it is dry. A finger poked into it will feel cold and wet, but no moisture will cling to that finger when it's lifted out of the mercury. A blob of mercury can be poured onto a slanted surface, and instead of trickling downhill and leaving a wet, wiggly track as other liquids do, the blob will roll along in one piece. If it should bump into something on the way, it will slide around the thing, like a blobby sort of animal looking for the easiest path. In fact, a blob of mercury behaves much like a living thing, which is why mercury got the name *quicksilver* long ago, *quick* being an old-fashioned word for "live." The name *mercury* comes from the name of the Roman god who was believed to be able to move with miraculous speed.

The alchemists of long ago regarded mercury as one of the basic ingredients of all things. Most of them believed every kind of metal was a mixture of mercury and sulfur in different proportions—and if they could mix just the right proportions together, they would make gold! Actually, cinnabar, the ore of mercury, *is* a compound of sulfur and mercury. When cinnabar is heated, the sulfur vaporizes as sulfur dioxide gas, which has a distinctive odor, leaving mercury behind. Perhaps it was seeing this happen that gave the alchemists their idea about sulfur and mercury.

Mercury in its many uses affects our daily lives. If you've ever had a fever, you probably had your temperature taken with a mercury thermometer. If the light switches in your house turn on and off very easily and silently, there's probably mercury in them. And if there are fluorescent lights in your home, they're filled with mercury vapor—mercury that has been turned into a gas which glows when electricity goes through it.

38

In ancient times, alchemists tried
to make gold from base metals.

Diamond — Gems and Cutting Tools

Koh-i-noor Diamond
in Persian Setting

PROUDLY, THE CONQUEROR strode into the throne room of the great palace. Generations of Mogul emperors had ruled India from this room, but now India had been conquered. Nadir Shah, of Persia, was India's new ruler.

As he swaggered toward the great throne that was now his, the Persian suddenly stopped short. The throne was adorned with jewels, and while jewels were nothing new to the Persian, here was one jewel such as he had never seen. It was an enormous diamond, flashing with sparkles of brilliant color.

"Kohinor!" exclaimed Nadir Shah. In his language, this meant "mountain of light."

For thousands of years, diamonds have been among the costliest and most precious of gems. Diamonds were first found in India, ages ago, and were eagerly sought by rulers and wealthy people of other lands. Some diamonds, such as the Koh-i-noor diamond named by Nadir Shah more than 250 years ago, have been famous for centuries.

Diamonds that are precious gems are mostly clear, colorless stones that seem to have sparks of many colors flashing inside them. The hardest of all minerals, a diamond will scratch glass, quartz, and iron and can only *be* scratched by another diamond. It hardly seems possible that such a hard, beautiful stone is formed of ex-

actly the same element as a chunk of black, crumbly charcoal—carbon. Of course, in charcoal the carbon atoms are loose and jumbled, while in a diamond they're tightly packed and evenly arranged to form the crystal shape.

Diamonds that have just been dug out of mines generally don't look a bit like diamonds you see in rings; they're usually dull and greasy looking. Only after they're cleaned and cut will they flash and gleam. Cut diamonds flash so brilliantly because light rays going into them are bent and reflected back out. Jewelers cut diamonds—using other diamonds to do the cutting—so that the crystal has many faces, or sides, to reflect light.

However, not all diamonds are clear and sparkling. Diamonds can be blue, yellow, brown, green, red, violet, or even black. Sometimes a diamond will be both clear and of a rich, deep color. Then it becomes an even more precious jewel, such as the famous Tiffany diamond, which is yellow. But most colored diamonds are pale or cloudy or have flaws in them and can't be used for jewelry. Only about 20 out of every 100 diamonds found is a gem; the others are used for making points for drills or for making special tools that can cut, grind, and polish granite and other hard substances.

Most diamonds are shaped like 2 four-sided pyramids stuck together at their

40

UNCUT YELLOW
DIAMOND

DIAMOND
OCTAHEDRON

DIAMOND IN
KIMBERLITE

BRILLIANT CUT
DIAMOND

UNCUT BLUE
DIAMOND

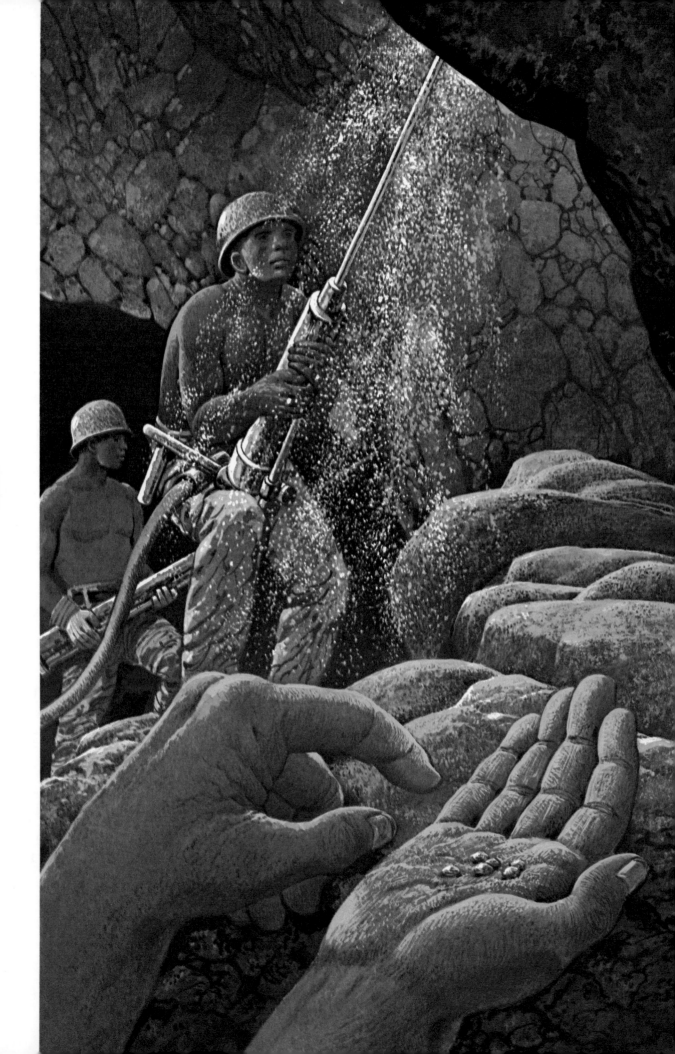

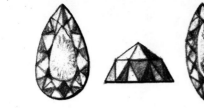

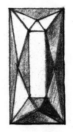

bases, an actual diamond shape. But some diamonds are nearly round, some are cube shaped, and some are combinations of four-sided pyramids stuck together at odd angles. Scientists think diamonds were formed when carbon was subjected to heat and pressure deep in the earth's mantle, long ago. They apparently developed in a bluish volcanic rock that was pushed up into parts of the crust. Many diamonds have been found in such rock, called kimberlite, in South Africa, where most diamonds now come from. However, in the past, a great many diamonds were found simply lying loose on the ground and in streambeds. They had apparently been worked out of their rocky nests by the slow action of rain and the grinding of glaciers, many thousands of years ago.

The largest diamond ever found weighed a bit more than $1\frac{1}{3}$ pounds.

Named the Cullinan diamond (after the president of the company that owned the mine it came from), it was found in South Africa in 1905. However, it was cut up into a number of smaller jewels, two of which are now the largest diamonds in the world and are part of the British crown jewels.

The Koh-i-noor diamond is said to have been found more than 5,000 years ago in India. It belonged to a number of different Indian rulers, who took it from one another by conquest! When the Persians conquered India in 1739, the diamond was taken to Persia for a time, but it was later brought back to India. When India became part of the British Empire, in 1849, the diamond was given to the British queen, Victoria. It, too, is now part of the British crown jewels.

Diamond is the birthstone of people born in April.

Opal — Fire in Stone

OPAL IS ONE of the few minerals that does not have a crystal form. It was not created by heat and pressure deep in the earth but was instead formed at the surface, or just below it, by the slow evaporation of thick, gummy, sandy water. It is often found lining cracks and cavities in rock.

Opal is quartz's "first cousin"; like quartz it's a compound of silicon and oxy-

gen. Unlike quartz, opal still has part of the water from which it formed held within it. As much as 20 percent—one-fifth—of a piece of opal can be made up of water.

Even though an opal is really nothing much more than sand and water, it may be awesomely beautiful. In some opal the silica forms clusters of tiny balls, and those clusters catch the light in a certain way and make the stone seem as if it were filled with colorful fire. Holding a piece of such opal in your hand is like holding a bit of a rainbow. Move your hand slightly, and the opal will flash and gleam with swiftly changing colors—glowing reds and purples, sparkles of brilliant green and yellow, and bright flashes of blue. A piece of opal of this sort is a precious stone, a gem; and as a matter of fact, the name *opal* comes from the word *upala*, which means "precious stone" in the ancient Sanskrit language of India.

Precious opal may be nearly transparent, milky white, dark blue, or gray. The dark kind is known as black opal, and it is the most precious and beautiful type, for its dark background makes the flashing rainbow of colors show up better. Black opal is a gem of our own time, for it comes mostly from Australia and was not discovered until 1905. Other kinds of opal have been known for thousands of years.

Because opal is porous—that is, with many tiny holes, like a sponge—and because there is water in it, an opal can dry out. This will cause it to lose much of its color and beauty, and it may even crack apart. On the other hand, an opal can also absorb, or soak up, moisture from around it, which may actually cause it to become stained. People who own precious opals really have to take care of them!

Of course, most opal is not precious. Common opal doesn't have any shimmering fire within it and so is worthless. A white or grayish kind of opal, too plain to be a gem, is found around geysers in many parts of the world and is known as geyserite. It often has the shape of an icicle or a lumpy cauliflower. Another kind of opal is found in huge cliffs formed millions of years ago by the shells of tiny sea plants. These plants, called diatoms, took silica out of the water and formed it into glassy shells around themselves. When they died, they sank to the sea bottom, and over millions of years their countless shells formed layers of ooze, thousands of feet deep. Today, those layers are cliffs of chalky common opal known as diatomaceous earth.

Opal is the birthstone of people born in October.

OCTOBER

MON	TUES	WED	THURS	FRI	SAT
	1	2	3	4	5
6 7	8	9	10	11	12
13 14	15	16	17	18	19
20 21	22	23	24	25	26
27 28	29	30	31		

Pitchblende — Mineral of the Atomic Age

IN THE CITY OF PARIS, one night in the year 1902, a man and woman opened the squeaking door of an old shed and went inside. Tiny, pale, bluish lights, like motionless fireflies, glowed in the darkness inside the shed. The glows came from glass bottles that contained a substance the woman had spent four years to produce—a new element that she and the man, her husband, had named *radium*. The couple stared in awe at the tiny glows.

The man and woman were the scientists Pierre and Marie Curie. In 1898, they heard that another scientist, Antoine Henri Becquerel, had found that the rare metal called uranium gave off strange "rays" of an unknown sort. When the metal was placed near wrapped, unexposed photographic film, the film became fogged as if it had been exposed to light. Marie Curie wanted to find out what the rays were and what caused them.

Uranium is a silvery-white metal present in tiny amounts in many kinds of rocks. But the main ore of uranium is a brittle, tarry-looking, brownish-black or grayish-black mineral called pitchblende or uraninite. Working with pitchblende, Marie Curie discovered that the mineral gave off a lot more rays—or radiation, as she called it—than could be accounted for by the amount of uranium in it. Clearly, something else was in the ore. Marie set out to find what it was.

She spent four years, working in the old shed that was her laboratory, slowly boiling down and refining an entire ton of pitchblende. Out of all that pitchblende and all that work, she finally produced a decigram—a little more than three-thousandths of an ounce—of radium, a metal element no one had even suspected existed. It was an awesome substance that gave off tremendous amounts of energy in the form of radiation.

The discovery of radium was literally the beginning of what we now call the atomic age. Scientists found that the radiation of uranium, radium, and other radioactive materials is caused by their atoms breaking apart. The nucleus, or center, of the atom shoots out tiny, tiny particles of itself in all directions at terrific speeds. This releases energy. Working with this knowledge, scientists have made discoveries that led to such useful things as nuclear power plants, as well as such fearsome ones as nuclear weapons.

Of course, as the particles in a uranium

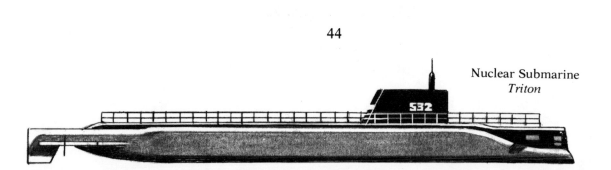

Nuclear Submarine
Triton

PITCHBLENDE
Canada

BECQUERELITE
Congo

AUTUNITE
Australia

ZEUNERITE
Germany

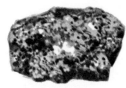

URANOPHANE
Utah

LEAD

nucleus fly off, the uranium changes into another element. It first becomes an element called thorium. The thorium continues to give off radiation until it becomes radium. The radium loses particles until it becomes an element called polonium, and the polonium loses particles until it has exactly the same kind of nucleus as lead—in other words it *becomes* lead. At this point no more radiation is given off, for lead is not radioactive. These changes do not happen all at once in a large quantity of uranium—it takes *billions* of years for a chunk of uranium to become lead!

The radiation given off by radium and other radioactive elements is dangerous. Large amounts of radiation entering a person's body can destroy cells that make up flesh, bone, and blood and can cause death. This was not known in the days when Marie Curie was working with radium, and she later died of a disease caused by radiation. Today, radium and other radioactive substances are kept in lead containers, through which the radiating particles cannot pass. People who work with radioactive materials wear special protective clothing and take great precautions.

No one knew uranium existed until a German chemist found it in pitchblende in 1789. And no one suspected there was such a thing as radium until Marie and Pierre Curie began seeking it in 1898. Today, these and other radioactive minerals are extremely useful in several ways. Doctors have found that small amounts of radiation from radium is helpful in treating the dreadful disease cancer. Uranium also is the fuel for nuclear power plants.

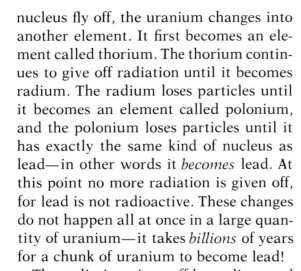

Protective clothing is worn in working with radioactive materials.

46

Corundum in Feldspar

Corundum — Rubies and Sapphires

A GLOWING, BLOODRED RUBY and a gleaming, cool-blue sapphire don't seem much alike, yet they're practically "brothers," for they're simply two forms of the mineral called corundum.

Corundum is a compound of the metal aluminum and the gas oxygen, and it's often found in crystals that look a bit like six-sided barrels. Common corundum crystals aren't a bit rare; they're usually bluish gray or brown, and rather cloudy. But if a bit of the element chromium is present in a corundum crystal, the crystal has the red color that makes it a valuable ruby. And if a bit of the element titanium is present, the crystal has the blue color that makes it a sapphire. Sometimes, corundum crystals have a rich, golden-yellow color, and these crystals, too, are precious jewels. Oddly enough, they're also called sapphires—yellow sapphires.

If you draw the six-sided shape called a hexagon and connect its opposite corners with straight lines, the lines will all cross in the middle, forming a six-pointed "star." Sometimes, a ruby or sapphire contains needle-shaped crystals of rutile, and these line up at angles to the six sides of the corundum crystal. Thus, they form a six-pointed star that catches the light. If the ruby or sapphire is cut and polished to form a smooth, rounded dome, it looks as if there is a gleaming star inside the jewel. Such a jewel is called a star ruby or a star sapphire and is very precious.

Naturally, such rare and beautiful gems as rubies and sapphires have a great many stories, legends, and beliefs associated with them. People once believed a ruby was red because there was fire inside it and that if a ruby were put into water, the water would boil! It was also believed that a ruby could cure certain diseases, stop bleeding, prevent its owner from getting the plague, and would even keep a person from being killed by a sword or spear. In China and other parts of the Orient, it was believed that inside a star ruby was a powerful spirit, which would bring great luck to the ruby's owner.

As for the sapphire, people believed that anyone who owned one of those blue jewels would always be healthy, rich, and strong; could never be overcome by enemies; and couldn't be kept in a prison— the sapphire would somehow get him out!

Ruby is the birthstone of people born in the month of July, and sapphire is the birthstone of those born in September.

Corundum Crystals

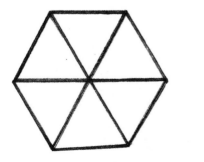

Star Shape of Rutile Crystals
in Ruby or Sapphire

Turquoise — Gemstone of Warm Lands

TURQUOISE IS A ROCK, and it's also a color that was named after the rock. The color turquoise is a greenish blue, but the rock may be sky-blue, apple-green, or even grayish, as well as greenish blue. Turquoise is a hard, shiny stone found in veins, chunks, and patches among rocks, most often in warm, dry lands such as Middle East countries and the southwestern United States. The name *turquoise* means "Turkish stone," because at one time most of the turquoise in Europe was bought from Turkey.

Turquoise can be polished to a smooth, lustrous shine, and people who lived where it could be found have always used it for jewelry. The ancient Egyptians made it into beads and bracelets and inlaid it into designs on wooden furniture, chests, and even mummy cases. The various Indian peoples of Mexico and the southwestern United States also delighted in making beautiful things from this pretty stone. The Aztecs of Mexico wore nose and lip ornaments of wood, clay, stone, gold, and silver; but only the emperor of all the Aztecs could wear a lip ornament made of turquoise.

According to an old, old legend of the Hopi Indian people, there wouldn't be a sun if it weren't for turquoise. This legend tells how the ancestors of the Hopi emerged from an underground cavern, long ago when the world was dark and unformed. They decided they needed a powerful light to illuminate the world, so they bleached a deerskin shield until it was pure white and painted it with shiny paint made from ground-up turquoise. Then they hurled the shining shield into the sky, where it stuck, becoming the sun!

As with most gemstones, it was believed throughout history that turquoise had magical properties. In ancient Egypt, it was worn as a protection against harm. In other parts of the Near East and Asia, people believed it would protect them against disease and bad luck. And in Europe, people had the odd belief that carrying a piece of turquoise could keep a person from falling off a horse!

Turquoise is a compound of copper, aluminum, a mineral called phosphorus, and water. It was formed by water trickling over rocks that contained aluminum, slowly building up crystals of the compound.

Turquoise is the birthstone for the month of December.

TURQUOISE
Arizona

TURQUOISE
California

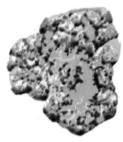

TURQUOISE
Iran

TURQUOISE
New Mexico

Arkansas Bauxite

Bauxite — The Ore of Aluminum

BAUXITE IS A ROCK that's a mixture of several minerals. It's not at all a pretty or interesting rock to look at; it usually resembles a chunk of concrete filled with tiny pebbles. Generally it's a drab brown, gray, yellow, white, or pinkish tan, depending on what's mixed in it. But it is quite an important rock, for it's the present source of all the world's aluminum.

Aluminum is a soft, very light, silvery metal. It was hardly used at all until about 100 years ago, but it's now the second-most-used metal in the world. Mixed with other metals, it becomes strong as steel, yet stays much lighter and can't be worn away as other metals can.

For this reason it's widely used for airplanes, automobiles, and storage containers. It's an even better conductor of electricity than copper and is used for outdoor power lines. You've probably seen aluminum pots and pans being used in your home, as well as rolls of paper-thin aluminum foil used for wrapping sandwiches and other foods to keep them fresh.

Aluminum is actually the third-most-common element on earth, and it is the most plentiful of all metals in the crust. However, it is always combined with other things, and bauxite is the only ore from which it can be removed cheaply. Bauxite is found above the ground, mainly in hot, moist areas of the world.

Sphalerite — Cymbals, Bugles, and Buckets

SPHALERITE IS A COMPOUND of zinc and sulfur and is the main ore of the brittle, bluish-white metal called zinc. It usually looks like a lump of many brownish or black shiny pyramids, cubes, or twelve-sided crystals stuck together. The crystals, however, are often misshapen and may be yellowish, red, or even colorless. Sphalerite sometimes resembles galena, the ore of lead. Its name comes from

a Greek word meaning "tricky," because ancient Greek metalworkers often mistook it for galena and were annoyed when they couldn't get lead from it.

Zinc is a useful metal. For one thing, when it's mixed with copper, the result is the shiny, golden metal called brass. Ancient peoples first made brass about 2,500 years ago, probably by accident. Once they knew how to make it, they used

50

it for coins, cooking kettles, and especially musical instruments such as cymbals and horns. The armies of ancient Rome marched to music played by brass trumpets, and today, many kinds of wind instruments—such as trumpets, trombones, and French horns—are made of brass. The portion of a symphony orchestra that contains such instruments is known as the brass section.

The main use of zinc is to coat steel and iron to make them rustproof. This is called galvanizing. Most metal buckets are made of galvanized, or zinc-coated, iron. Zinc is also an important part of flashlight batteries. Zinc oxide, a powdery compound of zinc and oxygen, is used in making soap and other products.

Nickel — "Old Nick's" Metal

SOME MINERS IN GERMANY, long ago, found what they thought was copper ore. But when they heated it to get the copper out, they obtained only a useless, lumpy, rocklike substance. The miners therefore decided the ore was bewitched and named it *kupfernickel.* In German this means "Old Nick's copper"—*Old Nick* being a name for the devil! Later a German scientist found a new element was locked into this ore, a metal that resembled silver but was hard as iron and wouldn't rust or tarnish. It became known by part of the name the miners had given the ore—*nickel.* And so, our name for the metal nickel actually means "Old Nick"!

Today, *kupfernickel* is called niccolite. It's a coppery-red mineral that does resemble the copper ore bornite but is a mixture of nickel and arsenic. Some of the nickel we use comes from niccolite, and some we get from a rather rare mineral called millerite, which often looks like clusters of shiny brass needles and is found in coal beds. But the main ore of nickel is the mineral pentlandite, which is a compound of nickel, iron, and sulfur. It's usually found as shiny, yellowish-brown cubic crystals in dark igneous rock.

Nickel has a number of uses. The United States coin called a nickel is a mixture of nickel and copper. Most "silverware"—forks, spoons, and knives—is actually a mixture of nickel, copper, and zinc covered with a thin coat of silver. But the most widespread use of nickel is in industry; it is mixed with iron and steel to make them tougher. The armor on army tanks is generally made of a nickel-bearing steel, or steel with nickel mixed in.

51

Nickel-Bearing Steel on M-1 Tank

More Rocks and Minerals

Amazonite (AM-uh-zuh-nyt)

Amazonite is one form of a group of minerals called feldspars, which are the most plentiful minerals in the earth's crust. All kinds of feldspars contain aluminum and silica, but amazonite also contains the element potassium. Amazonite is sometimes used as an ornamental stone in buildings.

Barite (BEH-ryt)

Barite is a compound of sulfur, oxygen, and barium. It is the main ore of barium, a soft, silvery heavy metal which is used in the manufacture of glass and pottery and also as a lubricating and cooling substance for oil drills. Barite crystals sometimes are shaped like a flower with open petals.

Autunite (oh-TUH-nyt)

Autunite is formed of uranium, calcium, phosphorus, oxygen, and water. It is an important ore of uranium. Bright yellow, or pale or dark green, it gives off a bright yellowish-green glow in ultraviolet light.

Bismuth (BIHZ-muhth)

Bismuth is an element. It is a silvery-white metal with a pink tint, sometimes found in veins in granite or gneiss rock but most often mixed in with other minerals. It is used in several kinds of medicines and is also mixed with some kinds of metals to make alloys—mixtures of metals—that melt easily.

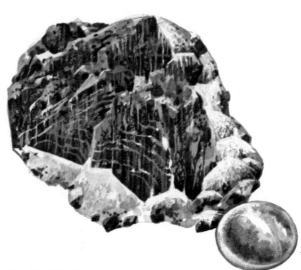

Celestite *(SEHL-uh-styt)*

Celestite is a compound of sulfur, oxygen, and the element strontium, which can be removed from the celestite as a silvery or yellowish metal. Celestite may be white, pale blue, reddish, greenish, brownish, or colorless, and either transparent or cloudy. It is the main ore of strontium, which is used in making paints, plastics, and fireworks.

Chrysoberyl *(KRIHS-uh-behr-uhl)*

Chrysoberyl is a compound of aluminum, oxygen, and beryllium. Chrysoberyl crystals are yellowish green. If they contain small amounts of chromium, they become the kind of gemstone known as alexandrite, which changes color according to the light—green in daylight and red in artificial light.

Cerussite *(suh-RUH-syt)*

Cerussite is a compound of lead, carbon, and oxygen. Often the mineral galena becomes cerussite as a result of the action of water containing carbon. Cerussite is usually transparent or smoky white or blue-green. It is an ore of lead.

Fluorite *(FLUR-yt)*

Fluorite is a soft mineral that often looks like transparent or cloudy cubes of colored glass. It may be yellow, pink, blue, green, purple, black, or colorless. It is a compound of the metal element calcium and the gas element fluorine. It is used in the manufacture of steel and aluminum, and a useful but dangerous chemical called hydrofluoric acid is made from fluorite.

Garnet *(GAHR-nuht)*

Garnet is actually a group of several minerals that resemble one another but are made up of different substances. Garnet crystals come in almost every color except blue. Some garnets are precious stones, and garnet is the birthstone for the month of January. Common, or nonprecious, garnet crystals are used for grinding and polishing other kinds of jewels and are also used in the machinery of watches.

Granite *(GRAN-uht)*

Granite is a very hard rock formed from a molten mineral mixture that cooled slowly within the earth's crust. It is made up of mostly quartz and feldspar. Because of its strength, it is often used in buildings and bridges.

Gneiss *(NYS)*

Gneiss is coarse, grainy rock formed out of granite, sandstone, or several other kinds of rock that were changed underground by extreme heat.

Idocrase *(YD-uh-kras)*

Idocrase, also called vesuvianite, is a brittle mineral that usually forms prism- or pyramid-shaped crystals. The crystals are generally greenish yellow or brownish but may sometimes be blue or pure green. When blue, they are called cyprine; green ones are called californite. Idocrase is sometimes used as a gemstone.

Lapis Lazuli *(LAP-uhs LAZ-uh-lee)*

Lapis lazuli, a rock formed of a mixture of several minerals, was one of the most precious gemstones to the ancient Egyptians and other ancient peoples. Its name comes from Latin words meaning "blue stone." The rich blue color in many famous paintings done hundreds of years ago was produced with paint made from ground lapis lazuli mixed with oil.

Margarite *(MAHR-guh-ryt)*

Margarite is a rather brittle mineral composed of calcium, aluminum, and silica. It is often found with corundum. Margarite crystals may be yellow, pink, gray, or green, with colorless streaks.

Manganite *(MANG-guh-nyt)*

Manganite—a compound of the metal element manganese, oxygen, and hydrogen—is often found in lakes and bogs. It is a main ore of manganese, which is an important metal used to strengthen steel.

Moonstone *(MOON-stohn)*

Two forms of feldspar, called oligoclase and adularia, often seem to contain a floating, cloudy light, like a moonbeam, and are known as moonstone. Moonstones are used as stones in rings and as necklace beads, and moonstone is the birthstone for June. An old legend says that the owner of a moonstone will find true love.

Muscovite *(MUHS-kuh-vyt)*
Muscovite is one of the minerals known as micas, which are formed from feldspar that was changed by heat and pressure. It splits easily into thin sheets that are springy, like stiff rubber, and that let light through. Such sheets were often used as windowpanes in medieval times, especially in Russia, which was then known as Muscovy. At that time, this mineral was called Muscovy glass.

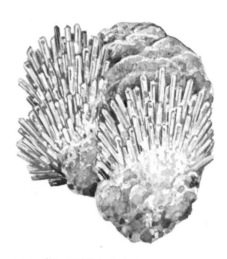

Natrolite *(NAY-truh-lyt)*
Formed of sodium, aluminum, silica, and water, natrolite is often found in clusters of long, barlike crystals on basalt rocks. It may be colorless, white, gray, yellow, or red, and either transparent or cloudy. It is often used for jewelry.

Obsidian *(uhb-SIHD-ee-uhn)*
Obsidian is glass that was formed naturally by a volcano. It was one of the first materials used for trade among prehistoric peoples, who prized it as an excellent material for chipping into weapons and tools.

Opal *(OH-puhl)*
Opal is really nothing more than a mix of silica and water, formed when thick, sandy water at, or near, the surface of the ground slowly evaporated. Much opal is merely whitish or grayish, but when a piece of opal has tiny spheres of silica arranged within it in a certain way, they catch the light, and the stone seems to have a host of fiery, many-colored sparks glowing inside it.

Orthoclase *(AWR-thuh-klays)*
Orthoclase is a form of feldspar containing potassium, aluminum, and silica. It generally forms in short, rather stubby bar-shaped crystals that are white or creamy pink.

Platinum *(PLAT-nuhm)*
Platinum is a rare metal element more costly and precious than gold. It is used for making jewelry but also is important in the chemical and electrical industries. It was first used by Indian people of Colombia, who made ornaments from it. Platinum is nearly always found mixed with other metals.

Rhodochrosite (rohd-uh-KROH-syt)
Rhodochrosite is a soft compound of the metal element manganese, carbon, and oxygen and is an ore of manganese. However, it is also often used for jewelry because of its pretty colors, which run from pale pink to deep red, as well as orange and brown.

Ruby (ROO-bee)
A ruby is simply a bit of the very common mineral corundum, a compound of aluminum and oxygen, that also has some chromium mixed into it, giving it a deep red color. The name *ruby* comes from the Latin word for "red."

Rutile (ROO-teel)
Rutile is a compound of the metal element titanium and oxygen. Red or reddish brown, it is sometimes found in clusters of needle-shaped crystals. It is an important ore of titanium, a strong but light metal used in making jet aircraft engines, surgical instruments, and many kinds of machinery.

Sapphire (SA-fyr)
A sapphire is a crystal of corundum, a compound of aluminum and oxygen, that also contains a bit of the element titanium. This gives it the lovely blue color that has come to be known as sapphire-blue. Actually, the name *sapphire* is from a Latin word that means "blue."

Schist (SHIHST)
Schist is a coarse rock that usually contains mica and quartz in layers and that generally splits easily into sheets.

Shale (SHAYL)
Shale is a sedimentary rock formed from clay and mud that were pressed together and hardened. It usually splits easily into thin, flat layers.

Spinel (spuh-NEHL)
Spinel is a compound of magnesium, aluminum, and oxygen. It is often formed in eight-sided crystals found embedded in limestone. When a crystal contains a bit of chromium, it has a rich red color and is used for jewelry. Red spinel has often been mistaken for ruby. Spinel crystals may also be blue, green, violet, or black.

Topaz (TOH-paz)
Topaz is a compound of aluminum, silica, and the greenish-yellow gas fluorine. It's found in large masses of coarse rock called pegmatite and was formed when hot vapors containing fluorine came in contact with compounds of aluminum and silica. Clear, golden-yellow crystals of topaz have been used as jewels for thousands of years. However, a topaz crystal may be cloudy instead of clear and may be yellowish brown, blue, pink, or colorless. There's even a very rare kind of red topaz. Topaz is the birthstone for November.

Stibnite (STIHB-nyt)
Stibnite is a compound of the metal element antimony and sulfur. It is shiny gray and sometimes forms clusters of long, bar-shaped crystals. It is the main ore of antimony, which is used for hardening and strengthening lead, as well as for many other things.

Tourmaline (TUR-muh-luhn)
Tourmaline, often used as a gemstone, is a mixture of many different elements. It forms in bar-shaped crystals embedded in rock. These crystals may be pink, red, blue, yellow, brown, green, black, or colorless. Pink tourmaline is the birthstone for October, as is opal.

Vivianite *(VIV-ee-uh-nyt)*
Vivianite is formed of iron, phosphorus, oxygen, and water. It is transparent or cloudy and is colorless when first dug up. Quickly, however, it becomes green, blue, purple, or black due to the iron in it combining with oxygen in the air. Vivianite is often one of the minerals found in the fossil bones of prehistoric animals.

Zincite *(ZING-kyt)*
Zincite, an ore of zinc, is a compound of zinc and oxygen. Zincite crystals are orange-yellow to deep red and are sometimes used in jewelry. This mineral is rather rare; it is found mainly in one part of New Jersey.

Wulfenite *(WUL-fuh-nyt)*
Wulfenite is formed of lead, oxygen, and the metal element called molybdenum. Wulfenite crystals are usually thin and squarish and a shiny yellow, orange, red, gray, white, olive-green, or brown. Wulfenite is a main ore of molybdenum, which is a strong, heat-resistant metal with many uses.

Zircon *(ZUHR-kahn)*
Zircon is formed of the metal element zirconium and silica but nearly always also has some of the metal element hafnium in it. It is the main source of zirconium, which is used for building parts of nuclear power plants. Zircon crystals, however, which may be red, brown, green, yellow, or colorless, are often used in jewelry. Blue zircon is the birthstone for December, as is turquoise.

Index

Italic page numbers indicate color illustrations.

Pronunciation Guide

aborigine	ab-uh-RIHJ-uh-nee
alchemist	AL-kuh-muhst
amethyst	AM-uh-thihst
bauxite	BAWK-syt
becquerelite	beh-KREH-lyt
beryl	BEHR-uhl
cassiterite	kuh-SIHT-uh-ryt
cerargyrite	suh-RAHR-juh-ryt
chalcedony	kal-SEHD-n-ee
chalcocite	KAL-kuh-syt
chalcopyrite	kal-kuh-PY-ryt
citrine	sih-TREEN
diatomaceous	dy-uht-uh-MAY-shuhs
galena	guh-LEE-nuh
geothite	GUH-tyt
graphite	GRA-fyt
igneous	IHG-nee-uhs
jadeite	JAY-dyt
Koh-i-noor	KOH-uh-nur
malachite	MAL-uh-kyt
metamorphic	meht-uh-MAWR-fihk
molybdenum	muh-LIHB-duh-nuhm
nephrite	NEHF-ryt
ocher	OH-kuhr
octahedron	ahk-tuh-HEE-druhn
oligoclase	OH-lih-goh-klays
piezoelectric	pee-ay-zoh-uh-LEHK-trihk
pyrite	PY-ryt
quartz	KWAWRTZ
sphalerite	SFAL-uh-ryt
turquoise	TUHR-koyz
vermiculite	vuhr-MIHK-yuh-lyt
zeunerite	ZOY-nuh-ryt

DURING the mid-afternoon of Wednesday, October 26, 1881, the Earp brothers - Virgil, Wyatt, and Morgan - and Doc Holliday walked northwest on Fremont Street toward the O.K. Corral. Their stated purpose was to disarm the cowboys hanging about the area. The mission was most likely to settle a personal score between the Earps and Holliday and the Clanton faction. As they neared their intended prey, Cochise County Sheriff John Behan tried to persuade the Earps to turn back, claiming he had disarmed the Clantons and McLaurys.

Clad in long black coats, the party moved on, ignoring Sheriff Behan as they passed. Boxed in by buildings, the Clantons, Ike and Billy, and the McLaurys, Tom and Frank, had one choice - fight. Virgil Earp, in his role as Tombstone's City Marshall, demanded the McLaurys and Clantons throw down their weapons and throw up their arms. Fear and tension permeated the air, within thirty seconds the feud was launched to a new level and silence replaced the rapid sound of gunfire. Tom and Frank McLaury and Billy Clanton lay in the street, their bodies riddled from bullets. Virgil and Morgan Earp and Holliday suffered wounds from Billy Clanton's and Frank McLaury's wild gunfire.

Recollections of the events that occurred that legendary afternoon vary, but those same accounts agree upon one thing - either Wyatt or Morgan fired first and deliberately, offering the Clantons and McLaurys little opportunity to obey Virgil's order. Morgan Earp, anxious to draw blood, shot Billy Clanton in the chest. Seconds earlier, Billy had begged "don't shoot!" and declared that

he did not want to fight. Severely wounded and laying on his back, Billy propped his gun on his knee and fired off round after round until the chamber of his Smith and Wesson was empty and his body too weak to continue the battle.

Because Frank McLaury was considered the best shot, Wyatt immediately shot him in the stomach. Grabbing his gut, Frank staggered into the street, sending off wild rounds from his gun. A slug from Morgan's gun caught Frank just below his right ear. The cowboy was dead before hitting the ground.

During the melee, Ike Clanton ran up to Wyatt, grabbed his left arm, and implored him to stop shooting. The lawman replied: "The fighting has commenced, go to fighting or get away." Ike Clanton fled the scene, taking cover at the adjacent photography gallery. Tom McLaury, unarmed, hid behind his horse. Holliday took aim and, when Tom's horse shied, blasted McLaury with buckshot. The cowboy staggered a few steps and collapsed.

Wyatt Earp and Doc Holliday were arrested for murder. A preliminary hearing cleared the men of any wrongdoing.

O.K. Corral, Tombstone, Arizona

ON March 19, 1848, Wyatt Earp, the third son of Nicholas and Virginia Earp was born in Monmouth, Illinois. The Earp family moved from Illinois to Missouri to Iowa before finally settling in California. Working as a laborer on the railroad, Wyatt made his way back to Lamar, Missouri.

In 1870, Wyatt was elected town constable, a position his half-brother, Newton, was also seeking. That same year Wyatt married his first wife, Urilla Sutherland. Three months after they married, Urilla died either from a typhoid epidemic or in childbirth. Whatever the cause, Urilla's family blamed Wyatt for her death.

Devastated by his loss, Wyatt drifted to Kansas and started a new life. He tried his hand at several occupations - buffalo hunter, horse thief, and gambler - before returning to law enforcement. In these various capacities, he met and befriended a small circle of friends that, like himself, became Western legends.

Wyatt began his career as law officer in 1875 while living in Wichita, Kansas. A series of misunderstandings, such as not turning in fines collected from prostitutes, resulted in his dismissal from the Wichita police force. The city fathers also requested that he and his brother, Morgan, find a new place to live. From Wichita, the Earps moved on to Dodge City where Wyatt secured a police officer position. In 1878, he became the city's assistant marshal.

During the three years spent in Dodge City, Wyatt became widely known as a brave and fearless police officer. He also met his second wife, Mattie, while living there.

In September 1879, Wyatt and Mattie left Dodge City for Las Vegas, New Mexico. There they joined other members of the Earp family and Doc Holliday. A few months later, the Earp brothers - Wyatt, Morgan, and Virgil - decided to move their families to Tombstone, Arizona.

Tombstone was only ten months old when the Earps and Doc Holliday arrived. Being a mining town, Tombstone presented opportunities to make a lot of money fast, especially through gambling. Wyatt immediately acquired an interest in the Oriental Saloon dealing faro. Certain events played out that resulted in the Earp brothers becoming lawmen. Virgil was appointed town marshall; Morgan and Wyatt served on the police force.

The Earps' monopoly on law enforcement immediately earned them the enmity of the Cowboy faction, who had the sympathy of Cochise County Sheriff, John Behan. Because the Earps interfered with rustling and stage robbing activities carried out by the Cowboys, in particular the Clanton faction, their presence in Tombstone was not welcomed.

Wyatt complicated matters further when he left Mattie for another women - Josephine Marcus. Josie

Wyatt Earp at age eighty

was the love interest of John Behan. Legend suggests that Josie was an actress at the Bird Cage Theatre and the two became infatuated with the other soon after she arrived in Tombstone. After Wyatt left Mattie, she became a prostitute and at the age of thirty committed suicide. Josie and Wyatt married in 1882.

Following the O.K. Corral gunfight, Wyatt continued the feud against the Cowboys. Seeking revenge for the attack on Virgil and the murder of Morgan,

Wyatt, Doc, and other Earp supporters hunted down and killed members of the Clanton faction.

After 1884, Wyatt gave up law enforcement and turned to other interests. Moving to various mining towns throughout the West, Wyatt pursued several endeavors; he owned saloons, prospected for gold, and raised thoroughbred horses. At the age of eighty, Wyatt died in 1929 while living in California.

ORGAN EARP, the younger brother of Wyatt and Virgil Earp, was born on April 24, 1851, at Pella, Iowa. The family moved to California in 1864. At the age of nineteen, he joined his brothers in Missouri.

After Wyatt's wife died in 1870, the brothers drifted to Kansas. In September 1875, the Wichita police arrested Morgan for an unnamed infraction. Seven months later, city officials ran him out of town for vagrancy.

After a brief stay in Deadwood, South Dakota, Morgan moved on to Butte, Montana, where he was the local marshal. True to the transitory nature of the Earp clan, Morgan did not stay in Montana long; he and his wife, Lou, returned to Kansas. Before joining the other Earp family members in Tombstone, Arizona, he served as Ford County deputy sheriff.

The first position Morgan held in Tombstone was shotgun guard for Wells Fargo. He resigned from the position to deal faro at the Occidental Saloon, but continued to play a role in law enforcement.

A bungled stage holdup and murder elevated the animosity between the Earp brothers and the Clanton faction. Morgan captured a local ruffian, Luther King, who identified the felons as members of the Clanton faction.

Tension between the Earps and Holliday and the Clanton faction reached an explosive point. The day before the O.K. Corral gunfight Morgan backed up Doc Holliday in an exchange of threats between the Clantons and Holliday. Some accounts of the gunfight claim Morgan fired the first shot, striking Billy Clanton in the chest area.

On March 18, 1882, at Hatch's Billiard Parlor, Morgan was shot twice while chalking up his cue. A large group of men, including Wyatt, were present when the assailants struck. The first slug entered the right side of his stomach, shattering his spinal col-

Morgan Earp, 1881

umn. Upon exiting its intended victim, the slug hit an onlooker causing a minor injury. The second shot struck Morgan in the side, whizzing pass Wyatt as he went to his brother's aid. Wyatt, with the help of two other men, stretched the dying man out on the billiard table. Three doctors were summoned, all agreed Morgan would not survive. Surrounded by his brothers and the Earp women, Morgan died less than an hour after being shot. His murder was believed to be a revenge killing carried out by Clanton sympathizers. Virgil and the Earp women took Morgan's body to California for burial.

DEPUTY
SHERIFF

4

HE second of seven children born to Nicholas and Virginia Earp, Virgil was born on July 18, 1843, at Hartford, Kentucky. When Virgil was a boy, the family moved to Illinois then Iowa. When the Civil War broke out, Virgil was eighteen years old. He enlisted with the Union army and served for the duration of the war.

After the war, Virgil returned to Iowa where he drove a stagecoach out of Council Bluffs. He and his second wife, Allie, moved to Kansas in 1870. (When Virgil was seventeen, he ran off with a sixteen-year-old girl. The girl's parents had the marriage annulled even though she bore him a daughter.) The Earps set up housekeeping in Dodge City, Kansas. Virgil served on the Dodge City police force.

During the mid-1870s, Virgil and Allie relocated to Prescott, Arizona. While living in Prescott, Virgil tried his hand at several occupations - farmer, mail carrier, and gold prospector.

Virgil Earp

In late 1879, Virgil and Allie left Prescott for Tombstone, Arizona. Virgil worked a number of odd jobs before he was appointed Deputy U.S. Marshal in 1880 (some accounts state Virgil received the appointment before going to Tombstone). On the evening of October 28, 1880, Tombstone marshal, Fred White, deputized Virgil to assist in arresting Curly Bill Brocius, a drunk cowboy. During a struggle between the men, Brocius' gun accidentally discharged, mortally wounding Marshal White. Upon White's death and until an election could be held, Virgil was temporarily appointed city marshal.

Virgil lost his first bid for city marshal. In June 1881, the citizens of Tombstone shifted their support to Virgil and elected him to the post, just as tension began to develop between the Earps and Clanton faction.

On the evening of October 25, 1881, Virgil played poker with Ike Clanton, Tom McLaury, and two other men. When the all-night card game ended, Virgil and Ike exchanged words. Virgil clubbed Ike in the head with his gun and dragged him to night court. Ike was fined and released, setting in motion the famed gunfight that occurred later that day, October 26th. Because of his involvement in the gunfight, Virgil was discharged from the marshal's position.

In a revenge motivated action, Virgil was ambushed the night of December 28, 1881, as he walked home from the Oriental Saloon. Buckshot wounds to his left side, arm, and back proved not to be fatal, but Virgil did lose the use of his left arm.

After Morgan's murder in 1882, Virgil and Allie went to California where he convalesced at the home of his parents. Four years later, Virgil opened a detective agency in Colton, California, only to abandon it for Arizona's goldfields. He returned to Colton and served as city marshal, but was again struck with a case of gold fever. In 1905, Virgil caught pneumonia while seeking his fortune and died at Goldfield, Nevada.

THE son of a prosperous Southern family, John Henry Holliday was born on August 14, 1851, in Griffin, Georgia. Because of his family's social status, John was required to choose a profession. In 1870, he enrolled in dental school at the Pennsylvania College of Dental Surgery. After completing the mandatory courses, Holliday received the degree of Doctor of Dental Surgery on March 1, 1872.

From Philadelphia he traveled to Atlanta, Georgia, and opened a dental practice. During this time, he contracted tuberculosis. Hoping to improve and extend his life, Holliday moved west. In 1873, he opened a practice in Dallas, Texas, but patients found his coughing fits uncomfortable and business soon dropped off.

J.H. (Doc) Holliday, as he appeared in the early eighties

Doc possessed a natural ability for gambling, a respectable but dangerous occupation. Armed with a gun in a shoulder holster, one on his hip, and a knife, Holliday soon acquired a gunfighter's reputation. Usually with a posse not far behind, a deadly temper kept him on the move.

In Fort Griffin, Texas, Doc met his only love interest, a prostitute named Big Nose Kate. She and Doc met while he was dealing cards at a local saloon owned by John Shanssey (Doc met Wyatt Earp at the same saloon). A confrontation over card game rules with a local ruffian, Ed Bailey, resulted in Bailey's death. Declaring he had acted in self- defense, Doc chose not to leave Fort Griffin and was promptly arrested. Angry over the murder of a local boy, Doc soon became the target of vigilante justice. Kate, well aware of Doc's predicament, diverted the crowd by setting an old shed on fire. The flames threatened to engulf the entire town. With everyone's attention turned on the fire, Kate entered the jail, disarmed the guard, and freed Doc. Together they headed for Dodge City, thus, the beginning of their turbulent relationship.

Kate and Doc joined the Earps in Tombstone, Arizona. On March 5, 1881, masked bandits attempted to rob a stagecoach after it had departed from Tombstone. Bud Philpot, the driver was shot and died instantly. The community of Tombstone was outraged over the incident. Although it was generally believed the Clanton faction was behind the failed robbery, Doc was implicated in the murder and rumors circulated that the Earps had planned the scheme. In a drunken rage, Kate signed a statement declaring Doc guilty of Philpot's murder. Doc was arrested, but later cleared of the charges. This accusation was a source of conflict that led up to the O.K. Corral gunfight. After the murder of Morgan Earp, Doc was a member of Wyatt's "posse" that eliminated those responsible for the attacks on the Earps.

Weak from tuberculosis and alcoholism, Doc checked into a sanitarium in Glenwood Springs, Colorado. At the age of thirty-five, the gunfighter died.

Doc Hollidays grave inscription: "He died in bed"

NEWMAN HAYNES "Old Man" Clanton, patriarch of the Clanton faction, moved his family from California to Arizona in 1873 and started his own farm community called "Clantonville" located in the Gila Valley. For four years the Clantons farmed the land without success. "Old Man" Clanton decided to try his luck at ranching and moved the family one hundred miles south to Lewis Springs, Arizona.

The discovery of silver and the founding of Tombstone created a demand for meat. To meet this need, Clanton built a large cattle empire. However, not all of the cattle purchased from "Old Man" Clanton was owned by the Clantons. A portion of his inventory was rustled in Mexico and brought over the Arizona and New Mexico borders. Before long, the Clanton cattle empire was aptly known as the notorious "Clanton Gang."

Besides cattle, "Old Man" Clanton invested in real estate. In Charleston, Arizona, he purchased two houses, a saloon, and various parcels of land. These real estate ventures were seemingly legitimate deals, but this new endeavor was not enough to prevent the elder Clanton's murder.

On August 13, 1881, Newman Haynes Clanton and four cowboys were gunned down in an ambush along Guadalupe Canyon. Several days prior to the attack on "Old Man" Clanton, rumors circulated that Clanton's men were the perpetrators behind the massacre and robbery of a Mexican mule train that was transporting silver bullion through Skeleton Canyon. Supporters of the Clanton faction suggested Doc Holliday and Wyatt Earp killed Clanton because of the need to eliminate possible witnesses that could tie Holliday to Bud Philpot's murder. Clanton's murder was ruled as a revenge killing carried out by friends and family members of the murdered mule train party. After Billy Clanton died, the two surviving Clanton sons traveled to Guadalupe Canyon and exhumed their father's body. Newman Haynes Clanton was buried beside Billy at Tombstone's Boothill Graveyard.

Patriarch of the Clanton clan, Newman Haynes Clanton

AHS #40882

BORN in 1847 while the family resided in Callaway County, Missouri, Ike Clanton was the third son of Newman Haynes and Mariah Sexton Clanton. Ike's mother died in 1866 leaving her husband to raise their four sons and two daughters. The family moved frequently before permanently settling in Arizona. In 1877 the Clantons constructed a large adobe house and began ranching near Lewis Springs. Ike helped with the ranch, but his interests were also centered on a restaurant that he opened the following year. However, the restaurant apparently did not succeed because in 1880 Ike had business interests in New Mexico. On November 26, 1880, Ike and gunfighter John Ringo filed a land location notice in Grant County, New Mexico. The partners named their 320 acres of graze and farm land "Simon Cienega."

By early 1881, Ike had returned to his father's ranch. When "Old Man" Clanton died, Ike took over as leader of the Clanton Gang. Besides cattle rustling, the Clantons were suspected of robbing stagecoaches. After Bud Philpot was murdered, Ike claimed Doc Holliday told him the details of Philpot's murder and confessed being the trigger man. Members of the Clanton faction were suspected of attempting the bungled robbery; Ike's accusation may have been an attempt to divert any attention focused on Clanton activities and rid Tombstone of the Earps and Holliday. The accusation resulted in Holliday's arrest. Although Doc was released and cleared of any involvement, Ike had earned the gunfighter's undying animosity.

On October 25, 1881, Ike Clanton and Tom McLaury drove into Tombstone to purchase supplies and enjoy a night of pleasure. Around 1:00 a.m., while eating in a saloon, Holliday approached Ike and challenged him to a fight. Claiming to be unarmed, Ike declined

Joseph Isaac "Ike" Clanton

the invitation. Ike and Tom spent the remainder of the evening drinking and gambling with Virgil Earp.

The morning of October 26, Ike armed himself and threatened to kill the first Earp he saw. Word of this reached Virgil, who approached Ike and arrested him for carrying a gun within the city limits. After paying a $27.50 fine, Ike was released. Outraged over his treatment, Ike made one final threat that set into motion the gunplay at the O.K. Corral. True to form, when the shooting began, Ike fled the scene. After the gunfight, he made three attempts to have the Earps charged with murder. His endeavors ended in failure. For that reason, it is likely that Ike Clanton orchestrated the attacks made on Virgil and Morgan Earp.

In 1887 Ike was caught stealing cattle. When he refused to surrender, Deputy Sheriff J.V. Brighton, with an aim sure and true, forever halted the cowboy's illegal activities.

HE youngest child of Newman Haynes Clanton, Billy, was born in 1862. At the time of his birth, the Clanton family was living in Dallas, Texas. Other than a minor encounter with the Earps in late 1880, Billy Clanton had managed to stay out of the lawmen's way. Wyatt had a horse stolen in Charleston, Arizona. When found, the horse was in Billy Clanton's possession. Billy gave the horse back and Wyatt forgave the infraction.

Of the Clanton brothers, Billy may have been the youngest but he kept a watchful eye on the reckless Ike. In the afternoon of October 26, Billy and Frank McLaury drove into Tombstone to collect their brothers. After hearing of Ike's arrest, Billy became agitated. Because he did not want to fight, Billy told Ike to return to the ranch. The Clanton and McLaury brothers were near the O.K. Corral on their way out of town when the Earps and Doc Holliday rounded the corner. Sheriff Behan attempted to disarm the Clantons and McLaurys. Ike and Tom were unarmed, but Billy and Frank were each wearing six-shooters. Virgil Earp ordered the men to throw down their weapons.

Accounts vary as to what happened next. Allegedly, Billy Clanton threw his arms up and shouted "Don't shoot me; I don't want to fight!" Within seconds, Billy lay on the ground with a bullet lodged in his chest. He returned the fire, emptying his Smith and Wesson until too weak to continue the fight.

After the gunfight, Billy was carried to a nearby house. As the nineteen-year-old boy lay dying, he cried that he had been murdered.

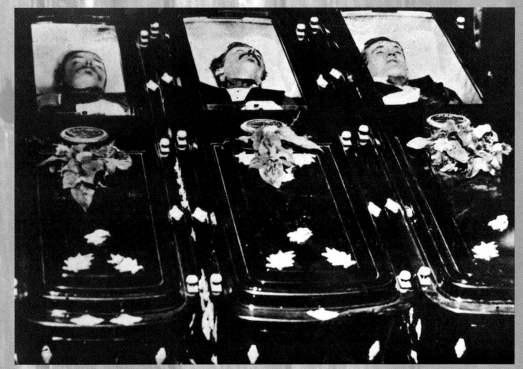

Left to right; Tom McLaury, Frank McLaury, and Billy Clanton. The victims of the O.K. Corral gunfight were displayed at a Tombstone hardware store prior to burial.

THE younger brother of Frank McLaury, Tom was born sometime after 1852 while the family was living in Iowa. Along with his brother, Frank, he settled in Arizona during the late 1870s. Tom worked the brothers' spread near Tombstone, while Frank hired out to neighboring ranches.

The McLaury brothers joined the Clanton faction in a widespread cattle rustling operation. When Doc Holliday was tried for his alleged involvement in Bud Philpot's murder, the McLaury brothers, out of loyalty to the Clanton family, testified against Holliday. The McLaury's accusation earned the resentment of Holliday and the Earp brothers.

On the morning of October 26, 1881, Tom and Wyatt Earp exchanged words. Wyatt drew his weapon and challenged Tom to a fight, which he refused. In response, Wyatt slapped Tom with one hand and, with his gun in the other, clubbed him on the head.

Not wanting any further problems with the Earps, Tom turned his gun over to Andy Mehan, a local saloon keeper. When Sheriff Behan later asked the Clantons and McLaurys for their weapons,

Tom McLaury

Tom pointed out that he was not armed. However, a Winchester was in the saddle boot on Tom's horse.

Before the first shot was fired, Tom shouted that he was unarmed. His declaration mattered little. Tom found refuge behind his horse until gunfire spooked the animal.

The horse shied, allowing Doc Holliday to zero in on his target. Twelve buckshot fired from Holliday's shotgun inflicted a fatal wound, penetrating a four-inch area on Tom's right side. Minutes after the gunfire ceased, Tom McLaury lay stretched out in a nearby house dead.

RAISED in Iowa, Frank McLaury was born in late 1851 or early 1852. He and his brother, Tom, settled in southern Arizona during the late 1870s. The brothers purchased two ranches and became associated with the Clanton cattle rustling ring.

Relations between the McLaury brothers and the Earp brothers were tense. Allegedly the feud revolved around a midnight encounter between Hattie Earp (the sixteen-year-old step-daughter of James Earp, the eldest of the Earp brothers) and one of the McLaury brothers. Another source of animosity may have centered around an argument between Doc Holliday and Frank McLaury over the quality of food served at Nellie Cashman's Russ House.

Whatever the reason, the dispute erupted on October 26, 1881. Frank rode into Tombstone with Billy Clanton during the afternoon. As he was leaving a store, Frank caught sight of Wyatt Earp pulling his horse by the bit. When Frank told Wyatt to let go of his horse, Wyatt pointed out that city ordinances prohibited horses being on the boardwalk, pulled the animal into the street, and dropped the reins.

An angry Frank McLaury retrieved his animal, rode to the O.K. Corral, and tied the horse up. Sheriff John Behan approached Frank and, hoping to prevent trouble, asked him to surrender his weapon. McLaury refused, claiming that he did not intend to start any trouble.

When the gunfight with the Earps broke out, Wyatt got the drop on Frank, shooting him in the stomach. Badly wounded, Frank staggered into the street and opened fire. Morgan Earp inflicted the fatal wound, striking Frank just below the right ear. The cowboy was dead before his body hit the street.

AHS #24.384

Frank McLaury

VERY little is known about the deadly gunman. Accounts regarding his date of birth range from 1842 to 1850 and place the blissful event somewhere between Indiana and Texas! Because he quoted Shakespeare and spoke Latin, Ringo was considered an educated man and may have attended college. Regardless of his alleged scholarly background, a sense of rage consumed the alcoholic gunfighter.

Charged with two counts of murder during the Mason County, Texas, range wars, Ringo was jailed in Austin, Texas. Ironically, he was cleared of the charges and elected constable of a Mason County town, Loyal Valley. The following year, 1879, Ringo headed west.

The grave of Johnny Ringo lies near the spot where his body was discovered.

After a brief stay in Shakespeare, New Mexico, Ringo found his way to Tombstone, Arizona. There he became closely involved with the Clanton faction. While rustling cattle for the Clantons, he also held a deputy commission under Sheriff John Behan. Although Ringo was not present when the hostilities between the Earps and Clantons took a deadly turn, he was thought to be connected with the December 1881 assault on Virgil Earp.

After going on a two week drinking spree with Buckskin Frank Leslie, Johnny Ringo's body was found propped against a tree in Turkey Creek Canyon, Arizona, on July 14, 1882. A single bullet hole to the head ended the gunfighter's life. Although ruled as suicide by the local coroner, mystery surrounded his death. According to legend, a search of the corpse revealed Ringo was armed with a pair of six-shooters and a rifle, all three weapons fully loaded. Plus, Ringo had been scalped. Friends of the gunfighter suspected that Wyatt Earp and Doc Holliday had a hand in Ringo's demise, but the suicide ruling remained the official cause of death.

Portrait of the Shakespeare quoting gunfighter,
John Peters Ringo

BORN on October 23, 1845, in Kansas City, Missouri, John Behan settled at Prescott, Arizona, in 1863. Behan quickly became prominent in the political realm and served the citizenry of Prescott through various elected law enforcement positions. In 1869, he married Victoria Zaff. The couple had two children, but the marriage was short-lived, ending in divorce six years later.

Behan moved on to Tombstone in 1880 and became sheriff of Pima County. Territorial Governor John Fremont appointed Behan to the newly created position Cochise County Sheriff, a position coveted by Wyatt Earp. Allegedly, Behan offered Earp an under-the-table deal. If Earp withdrew his name from the list of candidates submitted to Fremont, Behan would appoint him Under-Sheriff and not seek a second term, allowing Earp to win the office. Earp agreed to the terms, but after Behan won the appointment he reneged on the offer.

Behan realized that winning a re-election depended on cowboy support. As a result, the good sheriff reputedly looked the other way when a crime was committed. Clanton friends and supporters acted as Behan's deputies, orchestrating stage robberies at the same time they were sworn to uphold the law. Virgil Earp, acting in his capacity as Deputy U.S. Marshal, infuriated Behan and the cowboys when he arrested Frank Stilwell, one of Behan's deputies, and Pete Spence for robbing a stage. Ike Clanton posted bond for his friends. The Earp-Behan relationship was further strained when Wyatt won the heart of Behan's live-in love, Josephine Marcus.

After leaving Tombstone, Behan held the position of Deputy Superintendent of the Arizona Penitentiary. He also served in the Spanish-American War. On June 7, 1912, while living in Tucson, Arizona, John Behan died.

Cochise County sheriff John Behan and his wife Victoria

LUKE L. SHORT was born in Mississippi; the family moved to Texas in 1856 when Luke was two years old. The Kansas railheads beckoned the young man when he was a teenager. After a few years on the cattle trail, Luke decided to change occupations. In 1876, he traveled to Nebraska and peddled whiskey to the Sioux Indians, a federal offense which landed him under arrest. Short escaped from his captors and dropped out of sight for a couple of years.

After a brief career as an army scout, Short settled in Leadville, Colorado, where he embarked upon a lucrative gambling career. In 1879, he traveled to Dodge City, Kansas, where he dealt faro at the Long Branch Saloon. Short followed his Dodge City friends - Wyatt Earp, Doc Holliday, and Bat Masterson - to Tombstone, Arizona. There he was a house dealer at the Oriental Saloon. During a card game, Short killed a fellow gambler when he refused to abide by the rules. Cleared of any wrongdoing, he returned to Dodge City and bought an interest in the Long Branch Saloon.

A meticulous dresser, Luke Short adorned his five-foot six-inch frame with fashionable clothing that befit his occupation.

A group of reform-minded city officials tried to shut down Short's operation and run him out of town. Short telegraphed his friends in Tombstone for help. Known as the "Peace Commission," Wyatt Earp and Bat Masterson were among those friends that came to his aid. The dispute was peacefully resolved; Short received a substantial sum of money for his interest in the saloon and left town.

From Dodge City, Short went to Fort Worth, Texas, and purchased an interest in the White Elephant Saloon. Trouble was again on the horizon. Gambling became illegal in Fort Worth, forcing Short's operation to go underground. A former city marshal, Long-haired Jim Courtright, controlled a protection racket. Short refused to pay Courtright protection money and a quarrel erupted. The conflict between the two men continued even though Short sold his interest in the White Elephant. On February 8, 1887, Short and Bat Masterson encountered Courtright at a shooting range. Courtright drew his gun, but the hammer caught on Short's watch chain, allowing Short time to draw his own gun. A bullet to Courtright's heart resolved the dispute.

Luke Short left Fort Worth for the mineral spa at Geuda Springs, Kansas. While there, at the age of thirty-nine, he died from dropsy.

BORN on November 26, 1853, at Quebec, Canada, Bat was the second of seven children. His parents, Thomas and Catherine Masterson, moved the family from Canada to New York to Illinois before settling near Wichita, Kansas, in 1867.

Bat and his older brother, Ed, left the family farm in 1872, marking the beginning of their legendary careers. The brothers traveled first to Dodge City where Bat worked for the Atchison, Topeka and Santa Fe Railroad. Bat left the railroad to hunt buffalo. On July 27, 1874, he was among the hunters that fought off a large-scale Indian attack led by Quanah Parker at Adobe Walls in the Texas Panhandle. After the Adobe Walls incident, Bat scouted for the U.S. Army. On October 12, 1874, he was relieved of his duties.

Bat returned to Dodge City, opened a saloon, and turned his attention to serving the law. In November 1877, the voters of Ford County elected Bat as their new sheriff. Ed, also active in law enforcement, worked for the Dodge City police; in April 1878, he was killed during a gunfight. Bat continued to capture felons that plagued the area. Early in 1879 he was appointed Deputy U.S. Marshal, causing Bat to leave Dodge City. Several months later, Bat hired his gun out to the Atchison, Topeka and Santa Fe Railroad and led a posse of gunmen in a railroad dispute. The results of the November election did not prove favorable, Masterson lost his bid for sheriff in a hotly contested race.

Having lost the election, Bat left Dodge City. After traveling to Colorado, New Mexico, and Nebraska, Bat took up residence in Kansas City. In 1881, he joined several Dodge City friends - Wyatt Earp and Luke Short - at Tombstone, Arizona. Bat did not stay in Tombstone long; a younger brother, Jim, sent a telegraph asking for his return to Dodge City.

The younger Masterson was part-owner of the Lady Gay Dance Hall and Saloon. A falling out between the partners and a bartender resulted in a wild exchange of gunfire. After receiving Jim's telegraph and plea for help, Bat took the train to Dodge City. Arriving on the morning of April 16, 1881, Bat caught sight of his brother's antagonist. As he stepped off the train, Bat shouted that he had traveled over a thousand miles to settle the dispute and that he was ready to fight. A gunfight immediately began on the crowded street. When a lull in the gunfire occurred, Dodge City's mayor and sheriff appeared on the scene brandishing shot guns. The fighting stopped, Bat paid a small fine, and left Dodge on the evening train.

In addition to lawman, Bat was a noted gambler, newspaper writer, and sports promoter. He married Emma Walters in 1891 and eleven years later the Mastersons moved to New York City. Bat died while working as a sportswriter for the *Morning Telegraph* in 1921.

ROBERT LEROY PARKER was born on April 13, 1866, at Beaver, Utah. Robert LeRoy, simply called Roy by his friends and family, was the oldest of thirteen children. In 1879, the Parkers moved to Circle Valley, an area known for its lawlessness. It was there that Roy befriended a local ruffian, Mike Cassidy.

At the age of sixteen, Parker began riding with Cassidy's cattle rustling ring, working as his right-hand man. During a raid, Mike Cassidy killed a Wyoming rancher and was forced to leave the area. Parker took over the operation and, as an expression of admiration, assumed the name Cassidy.

Roy Cassidy expanded his operations to include train robberies, followed by a two year bank robbery spree in Denver and Telluride, Colorado. Shortly thereafter, Cassidy assumed the alias "George Cassidy" and took a reprieve from the life of an outlaw.

Quietly settled in Wyoming, he worked as a butcher in Rock Springs, thus the nickname "Butch." Like many of his contemporaries, Cassidy tried to walk the straight and narrow, but failed. In 1893, Cassidy was arrested for stealing a horse. For this deed, he was sentenced to the Wyoming State Prison. After an eighteen month stint, Cassidy received a pardon. The pardon had one stipulation, Cassidy was forbidden to pursue his line of work within the borders of Wyoming. Other places were apparently fair game. Upon his release in 1896, Butch formed a gang of outlaws known as the "Wild Bunch."

Robert LeRoy Parker,
A.K.A. Butch Cassidy

The "Wild Bunch" had a flair for dramatics. On June 2, 1899, using a warning lamp, the gang stopped the Union Pacific's Overland Limited and detached the express car. When the guard inside refused to open the door, a single stick of dynamite was ignited to gain access without harming the guard. Several sticks of dynamite were used on the safe, blowing it apart and sending currency flying through the air. The gang rode off with $30,000.

Although some of Butch's associates were ruthless killers, he avoided needless violence. When pursued by a posse, the horses, never the riders, were his target. Later in life, the outlaw claimed that he had never killed a man.

Eluding the law became increasingly difficult; by the turn of the century the "Wild Bunch" was wanted in at least five states. With Pinkerton detectives hot on the gang's trail, Cassidy decided to break up the "Wild Bunch." Following a short trip to New York, Cassidy, Harry "Sundance Kid" Longabaugh and his mistress, Etta Place, decided to ply their skill in South America. Taking separate routes, the trio reunited at Montevideo, Uruguay. From there they set out for Argentina and operated a successful sheep and cattle ranch.

South America proved not to be a safe haven from the scales of justice; Pinkerton detectives continued to track their movements. Sensing danger, Butch and Sundance decided to leave Argentina.

The Wild Bunch. Left to right seated: Harry "Sundance Kid" Longabaugh, Ben Kilpatrick, and Butch Cassidy. Left to right standing: Bill Carver and Harvey " Kid Curry" Logan.

They did not, however, depart empty handed or quietly - they robbed three banks in Argentina and a train in Bolivia. Etta fell ill with acute appendicitis, momentarily ending their criminal activities.

Etta's operation was performed in Denver. After a late night drinking spree, Sundance shot up his hotel room. To avoid arrest, Butch and Sundance left Etta and returned to South America.

The two outlaws worked at a Peruvian gold mine with periodic raids into Bolivia, robbing banks, trains, and stores. In early 1908, the Bolivian police caught up with them.

Legend claims Butch and Sundance died in a blaze of gunfire at a remote Bolivian border village.

Legend also claims Butch escaped and returned to the United States.

Using an assumed identity, William Thadeus Phillips, Butch passed himself off as a mechanical engineer from Des Moines, Iowa. The following spring he married Gertrude Livesay and the couple moved to Globe, Arizona where he was a mercenary in the Mexican Revolution. From Arizona, the Phillips went to Spokane, Washington, and started an office equipment company. In the early 1930s, Phillips sold the business, a move brought on by the Great Depression. Cancer, not a lawman's bullet, claimed the life of William Thadeus Phillips.

HENRY McCARTY was born in the east, possibly on Manhattan's lower east side near the present day site of the Brooklyn Bridge, in 1859. The McCarty family moved westward, either to Kansas or Indiana, during the Civil War. After the elder McCarty died, the boys' mother, Catherine, moved her family to New Mexico. In 1873 Catherine married William H. Antrim and the new family set up housekeeping in Silver City. Mrs. Antrim died the following year from tuberculosis. With their mother gone, the McCarty boys were placed in foster homes.

The first serious brush with the law occurred when McCarty was seventeen. At a Fort Grant, Arizona, saloon, Henry shot an Irishman who later died. A coroner's jury found the teenager guilty of murder. The Kid escaped justice by fleeing across the border into New Mexico.

Using the alias "Kid Antrim," McCarty found work at a ranch owned by John Tunstall, an unwilling participant and victim of the bloody Lincoln County War. Personified as a father figure, Tunstall's murder was for Billy a personal blow.

Seeking vengeance, Billy led a posse known as the Regulators. This band of young strays on the morning of April 1, 1878, killed Lincoln County Sheriff William Brady and his deputy George Hindman. In the months that followed, a series of running battles between the Regulators and the opposition caused minor casualties and attracted widespread attention. During the month of July, the Regulators waged a four-day fight in Lincoln. Billy escaped unscathed, but several of his companions were not so lucky. Several days later the Kid surrendered in exchange for amnesty from Territorial Governor Lew Wallace. Before the matter went to trial, Billy became nervous and left Lincoln.

Now a fugitive, the Kid formed a band of stock rustlers and embarked on a career of stealing and killing that spread from the New Mexico Territory to the Texas Panhandle. On January 10, 1880, at Fort Sumner, New Mexico, the Kid killed gambler Joe Grant. A posse from White Oaks, New Mexico, trapped Billy and two cohorts at a ranch owned by Jim Greathouse. When Greathouse was declared a hostage, Deputy Sheriff James Carlyle agreed to exchange places with him. Talks between Billy and Carlyle proved futile; around midnight Carlyle escaped through a window. A hail of gunfire delivered by both parties riddled Carlyle's body. Billy and his pals escaped.

At a deserted house near Stinking Springs, New Mexico, a posse led by Sheriff Pat Garrett arrested the Kid and his confederates on December 23, 1880. The courts handed down a death sentence; Billy's execution was set for May 13, 1881. While awaiting his execution at Lincoln, New Mexico, the Kid pulled off a daring escape that left his guards dead.

Sheriff Garrett caught up with Billy at Fort Sumner on July 14, 1881. At the home of Pete Maxwell Garrett shot Billy in the heart, killing him instantly.

Billy the Kid

THE son of a Southern planter, Pat Garrett was born on June 5, 1850, at Chambers County, Alabama. In 1856 the Garretts moved to a 3,000-acre plantation in Louisiana. Soon after the Civil War, both of his parents died.

Garrett left Louisiana in 1869 for the Texas Panhandle. Over the next several years he tried his hand at cattle punching and buffalo hunting before moving on to Fort Sumner, New Mexico. Prior to his legendary law enforcement career, Garrett first tended bar then opened a small cafe. In 1879 he married a young woman who died in premature childbirth. Shortly after her death, he married his second wife and started a family.

While living at Fort Sumner, Garrett and Billy the Kid became fast friends. At the height of the Lincoln County cattle war, Garrett was elected sheriff of Lincoln County. The newly elected sheriff's chief objective was to subdue his old friend and restore the peace. Garrett arrested Billy the Kid and his cohorts on December 23, 1880, at Stinking Springs, New Mexico. Billy escaped jail only to have Garrett hotly resume his pursuit which ended with Billy's death on the night of July 14, 1881. For his hand in the Kid's death, Garrett won both gratitude and animosity. Collecting the reward money posted for the Kid proved difficult; only after hiring a lawyer did Garrett acquire what he considered his just due. In an effort to explain his position, Garrett wrote a biography on Henry McCarty, A.K.A. Billy the Kid.

Before and after Garrett's involvement with Billy the Kid, he was involved in several gunfights. Near Fort Griffin, Texas, in November 1876, Garrett was on a buffalo hunting expedition. A remark made in jest to an Irish skinner, Joe Briscoe, was taken as an insult. Briscoe seized an ax and ran toward Garrett, but the Irishman was stopped dead in his tracks when Garret pumped a slug into the man's chest.

Settled on a ranch near Las Cruces, New Mexico, Garrett leased a tract of land to Wayne Brazel. A dispute arose between the two men when Brazel began to graze a herd of goats on the leased property. Tensions heightened when a third party became involved and offered to lease the disputed land. On February 29, 1908, the three men were riding together about four miles from Las Cruces. Garrett stopped his buggy to attend to some personal business. From behind, a slug hit him in the head and exited out above his right eye. A second bullet caught Garrett in the stomach. The former lawman died minutes later. His murder was ruled as self-defense and the perpetrator walked free.

Pat Garrett

ON September 5, 1847, at the James family farm in Clay County, Missouri, Jesse Woodson James was born. When he was three years old his preacher father caught gold fever and headed for the California goldfields, leaving his wife and children behind. Soon after reaching California, Robert James became ill and died. Zerelda James quickly remarried; the union lasted a few months. Her third husband was Dr. Reuben Samuel, a gentle man and kind father to her boys.

The Samuels aligned with the Confederacy during the Civil War. On several occasions, Union supporters abused James-Samuel family members. Jesse and his family also suffered at the hands of

a young Jesse James

Union soldiers; he witnessed the torture of his step-father and the maltreatment of his pregnant mother. In 1864 the teenage boy left home, joined Quantrill's Irregulars, and swore vengeance against anything Yankee.

Following the Civil War, Jesse continued the outlaw existence he had lived as a member of Quantrill's band. Through a series of bank and train robberies, he continued the fight against anything Yankee and sought revenge for the defeated Confederacy. The first postwar robbery Jesse and his brother Frank committed was on February 13, 1866, at the Clay County Savings Bank in Liberty, Missouri. An innocent bystander was gunned down on the street as the James-Younger gang rode off with more than $60,000 in the first daylight bank robbery (during peace time) in American history. Spanning a period of fifteen years, the James brothers robbed a dozen banks in seven states. The 1876 robbery of a Northfield, Minnesota bank proved to be the bloodiest.

On September 7, 1876, eight men clad in linen dusters rode into Northfield, Minnesota. Jesse, Bob Younger, and Charlie Pitts were the first to reach their destination - the First National Bank. While Frank and four other men cleared the streets of bystanders, Jesse, Bob, and Charlie stormed the bank. After spying the safe inside the vault, Jesse ordered cashier Joseph L. Heywood to open it. Claiming it could not be opened because of a time lock, Heywood risked a feign and toyed with fate; the cashier's throat was slashed before a bullet exhausted what life remained. A.E. Bunker, a teller, was shot in the shoulder as he escaped from the bank. After reaching safety, Bunker alerted the townspeople of the robbery. The citizens of Northfield reacted to this intrusion with a blaze of gunfire. Before Jesse mount-

Mrs. Zee Mimms James

ed his sorrel, two members of the gang lay dead. By the time the six remaining bandits reached the edge of town, the gang was decimated. Only Frank and Jesse escaped with minor wounds.

In 1874, Jesse married Zee Mimms, his longtime love. Within a few years the couple had two children. The family moved frequently, seeking refuge in Texas and Tennessee. Using the alias Thomas Howard, Jesse moved his family back to Missouri. At their home in St. Joseph, he was shot in the back of the head by a new gang member, Bob Ford, on April 3, 1882.

At the age of thirty-four the outlaw "hero" was returned to the family farm and buried. In a period covering a little more than a century, the body of Jesse James was buried a total of four times.

THE older brother of Jesse James was born at the James farm in Clay County, Missouri, on January 10, 1843. Frank joined William Quantrill's band of Missouri guerrillas in 1861 or 1862. Quantrill led a ruthless slaughter against the citizens of Lawrence, Kansas in 1863. Amid burning ruin, the lifeless remains of 150 men and boys lay while Quantrill and his men, including Frank James, got drunk. At war's end, Quantrill's Irregulars were refused amnesty for their indiscriminate acts of terrorism.

Hardened and well trained in guerrilla hit and run tactics, Frank and Jesse embarked upon a life of crime. In 1873, the James gang expanded their operation to include trains. On behalf of the banking community, the Pinkerton Agency had pursued Frank and Jesse since 1869. In 1874 the railroads sought the services of the famed detective agency. A plan was devised for a Pinkerton detective to arrest Frank and Jesse on their home turf. Under the guise of seeking work as a farm hand, agent John J. Whicher hoped to catch the James brothers at their mother's home. A local sheriff and a former banker cau-

The notorious James Brothers, Frank and Jesse

tioned Whicher of his folly, but he balked at the warning. The following day Whicher's body was found; Frank was suspected of delivering the two shots - one to the head and the other lodged in the heart - that foiled the detective's foolhardy plan.

On October 4, 1882, fearing he would meet the same fate as his brother, Frank surrendered to Missouri Governor Thomas J. Crittendon. After a series of trials and legal moves, Frank was acquitted of all charges leveled against him. In 1885 he was released from custody and returned home to his wife, Annie. For the next thirty years, Frank carried on an honest and peaceful existence working as a race starter at county fairs and a theater doorman. Frank James and Cole Younger reunited in 1903; the James-Younger Wild West Show enabled curiosity seekers to view the reformed outlaws. The James family moved about living in New Jersey, Texas, Oklahoma, and New Orleans, before returning to Missouri and the old family farm where Frank died in 1915.

THOMAS COLEMAN YOUNGER, born January 15, 1844; James Younger, born January 15, 1848; and Robert Younger, born October 1853; hailed from Lee's Summit, Missouri. At the outbreak of the Civil War, Cole joined Quantrill's Irregulars. In 1862, the

Bob, James, and Cole Younger with sister Rhetta.

father of Cole, Jim, and Bob Younger was murdered, probably by Kansas Jayhawkers. The brothers were outraged by their father's death.

Cole reacted to the murder by joining the regular Confederate troops, but continued his guerrilla activities. He soon proved to be a cold and ruthless killer. Curious how many bodies one bullet could penetrate, Cole tied several Yankee prisoners together, forced them against a tree, and fired an Enfield rifle into their backs.

Jim sought to avenge his father's death by joining up with Quantrill; he rode with the murderous marauder throughout the war. Captured with Quantrill near Smiley, Kentucky, Jim spent the closing days of the war confined to a military prison in Alton, Illinois.

With the war behind them, Cole and Jim returned to the family farm in Lee's Summit. In January 1866 Cole met up with Quantrill veteran Frank James. Cole was invited to join Frank and Jesse in the Liberty, Missouri, bank hold up. Jim grew tired of working the family farm and joined the gang. Bob soon followed.

The Northfield, Minnesota robbery in 1876 marked the end of the Younger's criminal ways. During the escape, Jim and Bob were badly wounded. With a posse in close pursuit, Jesse suggested Cole finish off Bob or leave him; Cole refused. Frank and Jesse split off and headed toward Dakota Territory. For two grueling weeks, a running battle took place between the Youngers and a posse. Even though they sustained numerous wounds, the brothers eluded capture.

Too weak to run any further, Cole, Jim, and Bob surrendered on September 7, 1876. Cole had been shot eleven times, Jim five, and Bob four. Rather than face the gallows, the brothers pled guilty to their crimes and received life sentences.

Bob died in prison, but in 1901 Cole and Jim received paroles. Under a new Minnesota law, they were free to leave jail but not Minnesota. The brothers sold monuments for the P.N. Peterson Granite Company and then switched to the insurance business. However, their criminal convictions invalidated the policies they had sold.

Suffering from depression, Jim checked into a St. Paul hotel and committed suicide. The following year, 1903, Cole received a pardon. After a stint with Frank James in the James-Younger Wild West Show, Cole traveled around the country lecturing on the evils of crime. He retired at Lee's Summit where he remained until his death in 1916.

YRA MAYBELLE SHIRLEY was born February 5, 1848, near Carthage, Missouri, the third of seven children born to John and Eliza Shirley. The Shirleys were staunch supporters of the Confederate cause. Therefore, when Myra's brother, Bud, decided to ride with Quantrill and his Confederate marauders, he received the ardent support of the entire Shirley family. Legend claims that as Myra watched her brother ride off, she vowed to harass the Yankees whenever possible.

Belle Starr and husband Sam Starr

During the summer of 1864, Bud was mortally wounded. The following day Myra made her intentions known; she wanted revenge and would marry the first man that avenged her brother's death. That same summer, Carthage was captured and burned by Union forces.

John Shirley moved his family to Texas; settling for a short time in Grapevine and Mesquite before making Scyene their permanent home. As in Carthage, Shirley opened a tavern and boarding house, which became a popular spot for ex-Confederates and war-hardened men. It was here that Myra, who preferred Belle, met and fell in love with the Bible-reading outlaw Cole Younger. If a relationship existed between Belle and Cole it was short lived.

On November 1, 1866, Belle married Jim Reed. The newlyweds moved to Missouri and lived with Jim's family. Either in 1868 or 1869, a daughter, Rosie Lee (Pearl), was born to Belle and Jim. After Pearl was born, Belle moved to Dallas and found work playing piano in different saloons. She soon branched out, gambling and dealing in stolen horseflesh.

Jim was wanted for a double murder and had sought refuge in Indian Territory. Hoping for a fresh start, Jim decided to move his family to California. While there a second child, Edwin, was born in 1871. They lived a happy domestic life in California, but trouble with the law in 1872 sent the Reeds running back to whence they came - Indian Territory and Texas.

A robbery carried out by Jim also placed suspicion upon

Belle. Around November 19, 1873, Walt Grayson was robbed by Jim and two accomplices. Grayson, a wealthy Creek Indian was thought to have stolen $30,000 from tribal funds. Three masked men approached Grayson and his wife, wrapped ropes around their necks, and threatened to hoist the pair up if they did not reveal where the money was hidden. Grayson talked, the gold was taken, and Belle returned to Dallas with a string of race horses.

A fellow outlaw, anxious to collect the bounty on Reed's head, murdered Jim in August 1874. Belle refused to identify the body making collection on the bounty impossible.

On May 15, 1880, Belle married Bruce Younger, first cousin of Cole Younger. The marriage was, however, short lived. Three weeks after her marriage to Younger, Belle took a third husband, Sam Starr, a member of the Cherokee Nation.

The Starrs set up housekeeping on the banks of the Canadian River in Indian Territory. Belle named their home Younger's Bend, a haven for outlaws seeking refuge. In the summer of 1882 Sam and Belle were arrested for stealing horses. After a four day trial, the Starrs were found guilty and ordered to the federal penitentiary in Detroit, Michigan. Described as model prisoners, they were released after nine months and returned to Younger's Bend.

On December 24, 1886, Belle and Sam attended a Christmas Eve party at the home of a neighbor. Also attending the party was Frank West, who had once arrested Sam. When West was spotted, Sam pulled his gun and forced a confrontation. Both men exchanged shots and died within minutes of one another. Belle again found herself a widow, but as before her state of widowhood was a temporary situation.

Husband number four, Jim July, was fourteen years her junior. This union was not a happy one; Jim was treated more like a son than a husband. Jim

Belle Starr, and her young friend, The Blue Duck.

was soon free of his domineering spouse. On February 8, 1889, Belle was riding home alone when she was blasted from behind with buckshot. The assassin was never discovered, but several men had motives: her son, Eddie; her new husband, Jim July; and an angry neighbor, Edgar Watson.

THE son of a professional soldier, Chris Madsen was born at Schleswig-Holstein, Denmark, on February 25, 1851. Before migrating to the United States in 1876, Madsen played an active role in European military affairs as a front line soldier. At the age of fourteen, he fought with the Danish army against German aggression. When hostilities between Denmark and Germany ceased, Madsen found a place in the French Foreign Legion. During the Franco-Prussian War he was wounded and taken prisoner. Confinement did not suit the young soldier; Madsen escaped prison and returned to the battlefield.

Madsen extended his military career to include the United States Army. Upon his migrating to the United States in 1876, he enlisted in the cavalry. Inadvertently, Madsen was listed among the dead at the Battle of Little Big Horn. Very much alive and well, he participated in Indian campaigns for fifteen years.

In 1891, Madsen resigned from the military and accepted a Deputy U.S. Marshal appointment. However, the Spanish-American War lured Madsen back to the cavalry. With the return of peace, the former Rough Rider returned to law enforcement.

Deputy Marshal Madsen was a member of the "Oklahoma Guardsmen," who were charged with halting the rampant criminal activities of Bill Doolin. Marshals Bill Tilghman and Heck Thomas rounded out the "Oklahoma Guardsmen" which marked the beginning of improved efforts to tame the Wild West. Although Madsen, Thomas, and Tilghman worked as a team, Doolin's known haunts were sliced up and each lawman assigned to a separate section. Under the direction of Marshal E.D. Nix, each lawman knew what the other was doing.

Madsen did not apprehend Doolin, but he did rid Oklahoma of a vicious Doolin accomplice, Red Buck George Weightman. On March 5, 1896, Madsen and a posse located Weightman at a dugout. Surrounded by lawmen, Weightman refused to surrender and tried to shoot his way out. With a single shot, Madsen killed the outlaw.

In 1911, Madsen was appointed U.S. Marshal for Oklahoma. Between the years 1918 and 1922, the governor of Oklahoma, J.B.A. Robertson, sought Madsen's service as a special investigator. Death found Christian Madsen at the Masonic Home in Guthrie, Oklahoma. The legendary lawman was approaching his ninety-third birthday.

BORN on July 4, 1854, at Fort Dodge, Iowa, Bill Tilghman began his illustrious career on the plains of Kansas. At the age of sixteen, he took up the life of a buffalo hunter. Well acquainted with the frontier and the people who lived on the vast plains, Tilghman proved a worthy scout for the army.

In 1877, he was appointed deputy sheriff of Ford County, Kansas. The following year, 1878, Tilghman found himself on the other side of the law when he was arrested twice for theft. By 1884, he had redeemed his reputation and returned to law enforcement. To celebrate his appointment as city marshal of Dodge City, Kansas, friends presented Tilghman with a badge made from two twenty-dollar gold pieces.

Tilghman and his family did not remain in Kansas; he staked a claim near Guthrie during the famed Oklahoma District Land Rush. The degree of lawlessness in the Oklahoma Territory enabled Tilghman to hold various law enforcement positions. Prior to his appointment as Deputy U.S. Marshal in 1892, Tilghman was city marshal of Perry. As a member of the "Oklahoma Guardsmen," he was instrumental in ridding the Territory of dangerous outlaw gangs.

Bill Tilghman, Chief of Oklahoma city police force.

In 1910, the voters elected him to the state senate. However, the following year Tilghman resigned from his legislative post to head the Oklahoma City police force.

To mark strides made by Oklahoma law officers, a motion picture, *The Passing of the Oklahoma Outlaws*, was released in 1915. Tilghman played a key role in the film's production. Christian Madsen and Tilghman spent the next several years promoting the film.

At the request of the citizenry, Tilghman left retirement to fill the position of city marshal of Cromwell, Oklahoma, in August 1924. On the evening of November 1, 1924, the aging marshal was dining at a local restaurant when a gun was fired outside. Tilghman stepped out to discover Wiley Lynn, a prohibition officer, drunk. Lynn discharged a shot from his gun while waving it around. A bystander wrestled the gun from Lynn and Tilghman proceeded to escort the prohibition officer to jail. En route, Lynn produced a second gun and shot Tilghman to death.

HECK THOMAS was born on January 6, 1850, at Oxford, Georgia. During the Civil War the young boy acted as a courier for Stonewall Jackson's brigade. Thomas married the daughter of an Atlanta preacher in 1871. A few years later, the family joined the westward trek, settling in Texas. Starting as a railroad guard for the Texas Express Company in Fort Worth, Heck advanced rapidly to chief agent. The local chief of police, Longhaired Jim Courtright, tutored Thomas in law enforcement.

Heck left the Texas Express Company and, after losing an election bid for the chief of police office, launched his law enforcement career. Employed by the Fort Worth Detective Association, Thomas tracked down and captured long-sought after fugitives. For his diligence, he was appointed Deputy U.S. Marshal under Judge Isaac Parker.

From Texas, Heck moved his family to Fort Smith, Arkansas. Hunting desperadoes in Indian Territory caused Thomas to be away from his family for extended periods. Unhappy with her situation, Mrs. Thomas packed up their five children, returned to Georgia, and filed for divorce.

Oklahoma guardsman "Heck" Thomas

Around 1891, Heck married Mattie Mowbray, a school teacher he had met three years earlier in Tulsa.

Headquartered in Oklahoma, Thomas turned his attention to the capture of the Doolin gang and other outlaws that openly roamed the country. Between 1893 and 1896, Deputy Marshal Thomas jailed more than 300 men.

One of Thomas' crowning moments was when, as one of the "Oklahoma Guardsmen," he trapped Bill Doolin. An informant tipped off Thomas as to where the outlaw might be found. Further, Doolin planned to take his wife and son out of the country. In the evening hours of August 25, 1896, at Lawton, Oklahoma, Thomas and his posse discovered Doolin hiding at a farm owned by his father-in-law. The posse found a well-stocked wagon, supporting the rumor Doolin was heading to Mexico or Canada. Hidden from view, the group of lawmen observed Doolin and his family emerge from the farm house. His wife and child boarded the wagon and the group proceeded down the moonlit lane. Thomas shouted for Doolin to surrender. The outlaw responded to the order with his Winchester. A posse member returned the fire, knocking the weapon from Doolin's hand. Along with another lawman, Thomas ended Doolin's career; his body was riddled with twenty-one wounds.

Around the turn of the century, Thomas held the chief of police office at Lawton, Oklahoma. Failing health forced the famous lawman into retirement in 1909. Three years later Heck Thomas died at the age of sixty-two.

BORN in Maryland and raised in Ohio, Isaac Charles Parker was thirty-six years of age when the jurisdiction of Western Arkansas fell under his charge. Prior to his move to Fort Smith, Arkansas, Parker had achieved an impressive record: St. Joseph, Missouri, City Attorney; presidential elector for Abraham Lincoln; judge of a Missouri backwoods district; and two-term representative to the U.S. Congress. Dubbed by his congressional colleagues "the Indians' best friend," Parker was concerned with the Indians' future. When he submitted to President Grant his application for the recently abandoned judgeship of the Western District of Arkansas, which included Indian Territory, it was not purely based on the need to clean up the lawless land.

Parker and his family arrived in Fort Smith,

Isaac Charles Parker, "The Hanging Judge"

Arkansas, on May 2, 1875. That same month he began his twenty-one year tenure as the law of the West. One of the first actions carried out by the new judge was the appointment of two hundred deputy marshals to police the 74,000 square miles that made up his jurisdiction. Armed with John Doe warrants, the deputy marshals had carte blanche to arrest and bring in anyone suspected of carrying out criminal activities.

Judge Parker held court from 8:30 a.m. until dusk six days a week; the court was his life. For the hunted desperado, the name Judge Parker struck fear. A guilty conviction in Parker's court many times resulted in a death sentence. Before his style of swift justice was questioned by the Supreme Court, Parker handed out eighty-eight death sentences. Of those sentenced, seventy-nine swung from the specially designed gallows, one killed in an escape attempt, one died awaiting sentence, and seven won reversals.

Aptly known as the "Hanging Judge," Parker tried 13,490 cases between the years 1875 and 1896. Not all tried in Parker's court were found guilty, approximately 4,000 suspects left the courtroom cleared of charges leveled against them.

In late spring of 1896, suffering from diabetes and exhaustion, Isaac Parker retired to his bedchamber never to re-enter his courtroom. He died in November. Before his death, the Western District of Arkansas was reduced in size. The dispensing of justice from the Fort Smith courthouse was largely responsible for the establishment of order west of the Mississippi.

HE unorthodox judge was born either in 1825 or 1826 at Mason County, Kentucky. Prior to dispensing justice in west Texas, Roy Bean was a trader, barkeeper, and smuggler. At the age of 56, he embarked upon his twenty year law career.

In 1882 at the west Texas railroad town of Langtry, Bean set up a saloon. Situated where the Pecos and Rio Grande Rivers join, Langtry was the gathering spot for about 8,000 railroad workers, gamblers, thieves, and rustlers that passed through the desolate country. At one end of the saloon Bean held court, while at the other end he served drinks and gambled. It was not unusual for court to recess so Bean could sell liquor or play poker.

Prior to receiving his appointment as justice of the peace, Texas Rangers brought prisoners to Bean for judgment. Self-taught in the ways of the law, Bean based his decisions on those statutes he found agreeable, all else was ignored. Since Bean found what he read difficult to understand, it is little wonder that his decisions were often odd and sometimes unfair.

In addition to barkeeper and justice of the peace, Bean was also the local coroner. On one occasion, a local worker plunged three hundred feet to his death. Having declared the man dead, Bean had to bury the corpse - a task he found most unpleasant. A brief search of the body produced $40 and a gun. In his judicial capacity, Bean found the corpse guilty of carrying a gun and leveled a fine of $40!

Fines levied for infractions of the law went directly from the guilty to the judge's pockets. Declaring his court was self-sufficient, Bean prevented an accounting of the court's records.

A picture of the beautiful English actress Lily Langtry claimed Bean's heart. Although married, Bean was deeply devoted to the English actress. In her honor, he named his saloon "The Jersey Lily." The law west of the Pecos passed with Bean's death in 1904.

Judge Roy Bean, seated on horse, in front of his saloon/courtroom.